Susan Muto

Words of Wisdom for Our World:
The Precautions and Counsels of
St. John of the Cross

About the Author

Susan Muto, Ph.D., is Executive Director of the Epiphany Association, an ecumenical spiritual formation center for laity, clergy, and religious, in Pittsburgh, and adjunct professor at Duquesne University and other institutes of higher learning. She is the author of numerous articles and books, including the series John of the Cross for Today *(Ave Maria Press).*

Susan Muto

Words of Wisdom for Our World: The Precautions and Counsels of St. John of the Cross

With a Preface and
Translation of the Saint's Texts by
Kieran Kavanaugh, OCD

ICS Publications
Institute of Carmelite Studies
Washington, D.C.
1996

ICS Publications
2131 Lincoln Road NE
Washington, DC 20002–1199

Typeset and produced in the U.S.A.

Acknowledgments & Permissions

An earlier version of Dr. Muto's commentary on the Counsels appeared in the Winter 1991 issue of Spiritual Life as "Wisdom For Today: The Counsels of John of the Cross." Cover design by Grey Coat Graphics. Painting by Gerardo Lopez, OCD.

Scripture texts used in this work are taken from the *New American Bible* Copyright © 1991, 1986, and 1970 by the Confraternity of Christian Doctrine, Washington, DC 20017 and are used by permission of the copyright owner. All rights reserved. No part of the New American Bible may be reproduced in any form or by any means without permission in writing from the copyright owner.

Excerpt from *The Sign of Jonas* by Thomas Merton, copyright 1953 by The Abbey of Our Lady of Gethsemani and renewed 1981 by Trustees of the Merton Legacy Trust, reprinted by permission of Harcourt Brace & Company.

Library of Congress Cataloging-in-Publication Data

Muto, Susan Annette.
    Words of wisdom for our world: the Precautions and Counsels of
St. John of the Cross/Susan Muto: with a preface and translation of
the Saint's texts by Kieran Kavanaugh.
      p. cm.
    Includes bibliographical references.
    ISBN: 0-935216-52-9
    1. John of the Cross, Saint, 1542–1591. Cautelas. 2. John of the
Cross, Saint, 1542–1591. Avisos. 3. Spiritual formation—Catholic
Church. 4. Catholic Church—Doctrines. 5. Temptations—
History of doctrines—16th century. I. Kavanaugh, Kieran, 1928– .
II. John of the Cross, Saint, 1542–1591. Cautelas. English.
III. John of the Cross, Saint, 1542–1591. Avisos. English. IV. Title.
BX2350.7.M89   1995
248.8'94—dc20   94-47484
                                                      CIP

TABLE OF CONTENTS

ABBREVIATIONS

Unless otherwise noted, all quotations from **St. John of the Cross** are taken from *The Collected Works of St. John of the Cross,* trans. Kieran Kavanaugh and Otilio Rodriguez, rev. ed. (Washington, DC: ICS Publications, 1991). In this edition, the *Precautions* and *Counsels* (as well as the *Degrees of Perfection*) are found on pages 719-729.

Biblical quotations taken from the New American Bible translation are indicated by the initials "NAB".

Preface

In the *Ascent of Mount Carmel,* St. John of the Cross is provocative: he stirs us to faith and prayer, but in many readers also incites anger because of his negative excess. Similarly, our first reaction to what he says in the *Precautions* and *Counsels* may be indignation. But what seems to prevent us from total rejection is the promise he holds out: holy recollection, spiritual silence, the peaceful comfort of the Holy Spirit, union with God, freedom. Those who make the effort find out for themselves, in varying degrees, how true the promises are. Then, too, someone will always remind us that Jesus himself had some equally hard sayings.

Nonetheless, in the case of the *Precautions,* the religious is likely to say that times have changed; and the lay person, that these things are meant for friars and nuns. Susan Muto, anticipating such responses, has directed her talents and learning to a deeper consideration of John's classic warnings, and urges us not to shy away from them. They can still make a powerful difference in our lives and be a treasure to every Christian who wants to live in the peace of the Holy Spirit. Since St. John's warnings are pithy and the general reader does not know their context, the kind of interpretation Susan Muto offers in the light of our present-day culture is a necessity. Her fresh insights illumine the text for our times.

I would like to preface her words with a word or two of my own about that context in which St. John of the Cross wrote these precautions. Their destinees were first the Discalced Carmelite nuns of Beas, a small town in the south of Spain. The community had been founded by St. Teresa of Avila. Living in the general area, at a monastery for Discalced Carmelite friars (1578-79), John of the Cross was asked by Teresa to be the nuns' spiritual director. He had already shown his talent for this ministry in previous years as spiritual director to the large community of over 150 nuns at the Incarnation in Avila in central Spain. St. Teresa wrote to the nuns in Beas that Fray John of the Cross was a "divine and heavenly man" and that she had "found no one like him in all Castile, nor anyone who inspires people with so much fervor on the way to heaven."

In addition to the personal attention John gave each of the nuns, guiding them in their individual spiritual lives, he was also teaching them through conferences to the community as a whole. These nuns were women influenced personally by St. Teresa and had ardently embraced the spiritual journey. Their love had little use for delay. St. John explained to them how to ascend Mt. Carmel quickly. The summit of the mount was a symbol for divine union with God. The path leading to it was the way of *nada* (nothing), for Christ had been reduced to nothing when dying on the cross. John explained to them the Scriptural basis and theological principles behind his teaching, and how the theological virtues of faith, hope, and love, working together in our lives, put us in relationship with Christ and purify or empty us of all that resists the Holy Spirit. In doing so they bring us into union with Christ and engulf us in his life.

As though this were not enough, he commented as well on his masterful love poem about the ardent exchanges between the bride-soul and Christ the Bridegroom. The poem bears the title *Cántico espiritual,* or "Spiritual Canticle." In this poem, the way is the way of love, and one of the stanzas has these words:

If, then, I am no longer
seen or found on the common,
you will say that I am lost;
that, stricken by love,
I lost myself, and was found.

St. John then explains: "Anyone truly in love will let all other things go in order to come closer to the loved one."

It was within this spiritual environment that the nuns received their director's *Precautions.* They understood their condensed character and particular objective in the light of John's personal care for them and his other writings. Indeed, they knew that union with God comes about not through the observance of precautions but by adapting to God's self-communication through the theological life of faith, hope, and love. John's *Precautions* take their value from their ability to promote this adaptation.

Christian spirituality, rooted in Scripture, has spoken often of three spiritual enemies: the world, the flesh, and the devil. Within this tradition, John finds the structure for his work: three precautions against each of the three enemies.

This little treatise became popular, and copies spread quickly, so that it was soon used among the friars too, as evident in the grammatical changes from feminine to masculine. Not long after, copies included further changes making them suitable for other religious and the laity. Not every change in these early copies came from John. But the value of the *Precautions* for anyone serious about the spiritual life must have been recognized quite quickly. John was a director sought out and esteemed by the people from all walks of life.

The text preferred by modern editors is the autograph copy made by Alonso de la Madre de Dios and conserved in the National Library of Madrid.

The *Counsels to a Religious on How to Reach Perfection* were written for a friar and are similar in content and tone to the *Precautions*. This suggests their having been composed about the same time. If they differ from the former work, they do so by not holding to its fixed structure. Some corresponding elements are obvious, though: the first counsel corresponds with the third precaution against the world; the second counsel, with the first precaution against the flesh; the third counsel, with the second and third precautions against the flesh; and the fourth counsel with the first precaution against the devil.

The copy that editors find most reliable was made from an ancient manuscript conserved by the Carmelite nuns in Bujalance. Appearing in the manuscript after these *Counsels* are the *Degrees of Perfection*, which past editors often placed among John's *Sayings*. The tendency now, however, is to leave them here since they seem destined for the same friar.

Kieran Kavanaugh, OCD

The Precautions

Instruction and precautions necessary for anyone desiring to be a true religious and reach perfection.

1. The soul must practice the following instructions if it wishes to attain in a short time holy recollection and spiritual silence, nakedness, and poverty of spirit, where one enjoys the peaceful comfort of the Holy Spirit, reaches union with God, is freed of all the obstacles incurred from the creatures of this world, defended against the wiles and deceits of the devil, and liberated from one's own self.

2. It should be noted, then, that all the harm the soul receives is born of its enemies, mentioned above: the world, the devil, and the flesh. The world is the enemy least difficult to conquer; the devil is the hardest to understand; but the flesh is the most tenacious, and its attacks continue as long as the old self lasts.

3. To gain complete mastery over any of these three enemies, one must vanquish all three of them; and in the weakening of one, the other two are weakened also. When all three are overpowered, no further war remains for the soul.

Against the World

4. To free yourself from the harm the world can do you, you should practice three precautions.

11

The first precaution

5. The first is that you should have an equal love for and an equal forgetfulness of all persons, whether relatives or not, and withdraw your heart from relatives as much as from others, and in some ways even more for fear that flesh and blood might be quickened by the natural love that is ever alive among kin, and must always be mortified for the sake of spiritual perfection.

6. Regard all as strangers, and you will fulfill your duty toward them better than by giving them the affection you owe God. Do not love one person more than another, for you will err; the person who loves God more is the one more worthy of love, and you do not know who this is. But forgetting everyone alike, as is necessary for holy recollection, you will free yourself from this error of loving one person more or less than another.

Do not think about others, neither good things nor bad. Flee them inasmuch as possible. And if you do not observe this practice, you will not know how to be a religious, nor will you be able to reach holy recollection or deliver yourself from imperfections. And if you should wish to allow yourself some freedom in this matter, the devil will deceive you in one way or another, or you will deceive yourself under some guise of good or evil.

In doing what we said, you will have security, for in no other way will you be capable of freeing yourself from the imperfections and harm derived from creatures.

The second precaution

7. The second precaution against the world concerns temporal goods. To free yourself truly of the harm stemming from this kind of good and to moderate the excess of your appetite, you should abhor all manner of possessions and not allow yourself to worry about these goods, neither for food, nor for clothing, nor for any other created thing, nor for tomorrow, and direct this care to something higher—to seeking the kingdom of God (seeking not to fail God); and the rest, as His Majesty says, will be added unto us [Mt

6:33], for he who looks after the beasts will not be forgetful of you. By this practice you will attain silence and peace in the senses.

The third precaution

8. The third precaution is very necessary so you may know how to guard yourself in the community against all harm that may arise in regard to the religious. Many, by not observing it, not only have lost the peace and good of their souls but have fallen and ordinarily continue to fall into many evils and sins.

It is that you very carefully guard yourself against thinking about what happens in the community, and even more against speaking of it, of anything in the past or present concerning a particular religious: nothing about his or her character or conduct or deeds no matter how serious any of this seems. Do not say anything under the color of zeal or of correcting a wrong, unless at the proper time to whomever by right you ought to tell. Never be scandalized or astonished at anything you happen to see or learn of, endeavoring to preserve your soul in forgetfulness of all that.

9. For, should you desire to pay heed to things, many will seem wrong, even were you to live among angels, because of your not understanding the substance of them. Take Lot's wife as an example: Because she was troubled at the destruction of the Sodomites and turned her head to watch what was happening, God punished her by converting her into a pillar of salt [Gn 19:26]. You are thus to understand God's will: that even were you to live among devils you should not turn the head of your thoughts to their affairs, but forget these things entirely and strive to keep your soul occupied purely and entirely in God, and not let the thought of this thing or that hinder you from so doing.

And to achieve this, be convinced that in monasteries and communities there is never a lack of stumbling blocks, since there is never a lack of devils who seek to overthrow the saints; God permits this in order to prove and try religious.

And if you do not guard yourself, acting as though you were not in the house, you will not know how to be a religious no matter

how much you do, nor will you attain holy denudation and recollection or free yourself of the harm arising from these thoughts. If you
are not cautious in this manner, no matter how good your intention
and zeal, the devil will catch you in one way or another. And you are
already fully captive when you allow yourself distractions of this sort.

Recall what the Apostle St. James asserts: If anyone thinks he
is religious, not restraining the tongue, that one's religion is vain
[Jas 1:26]. This applies as much to the interior as to the exterior
tongue.

Against the Devil

10. The one who aspires to perfection should use three precautions to be delivered from the devil, one's second enemy. It
should be noted that among the many wiles of the devil for deceiving spiritual persons, the most common is deceiving them under the
appearance of good rather than of evil, for the devil already knows
that they will scarcely choose a recognized evil. Thus you should
always be suspicious of what appears good, especially when not
obliged by obedience. To do the right thing, and be safe in such a
matter, you ought to take the proper counsel.

The first precaution

11. Let, then, the first precaution be that, without the command of obedience, you never take upon yourself any work—apart
from the obligations of your state—however good and full of charity it may seem, whether for yourself or for anyone else inside or
outside the house. By such a practice you will win merit and security, avoid possession, and flee from harm and evils unknown to you,
for God will one day demand an account. If you do not observe this
precaution in little things as well as big, you will be unable to avoid
the devil's deceiving you to a small or great degree, no matter how
right you think you are.

Even if your negligence amounts to no more than not being
governed by obedience in all things, you culpably err, since God
wants obedience more than sacrifice [1 Sm 15:22]. The actions of

religious are not their own, but belong to obedience, and if you withdraw them from obedience, you will have to count them as lost.

The second precaution

12. Let the second precaution be that you always look on the superior as though on God, no matter who he happens to be, for he takes God's place. And note that the devil, humility's enemy, is a great and crafty meddler in this area. Much profit and gain come from considering the superior in this light, but serious loss and harm lie in not doing so. Watch, therefore, with singular care that you not dwell on your superior's character, mode of behavior, ability, or any other methods of procedure, for you will so harm yourself as to change your obedience from divine to human, being motivated only by the visible traits of the superior, and not by the invisible God whom you serve through him.

Your obedience is vain and all the more fruitless in the measure that you allow the superior's unpleasant character to annoy you or his good and pleasing manners to make you happy. For I tell you that by inducing religious to consider these modes of conduct, the devil has ruined a vast number of them in their journey toward perfection. Their acts of obedience are worth little in God's sight, since they allow these considerations to interfere with obedience.

If you do not strive, with respect to your personal feelings, to be unconcerned about whether this one or another be superior, you will by no means be a spiritual person, nor will you keep your vows well.

The third precaution

13. The third precaution, directly against the devil, is that you ever seek with all your heart to humble yourself in word and in deed, rejoicing in the good of others as if it were your own, desiring that they be given precedence over you in all things; and this you should do wholeheartedly. You will thereby overcome evil with good [Rom 12:21], banish the devil, and possess a happy heart. Try to practice this more with those who least attract you. Realize that if you do not

train yourself in this way, you will not attain real charity or make any progress in it.

And ever prefer to be taught by all rather than desire to teach even the least of all.

Against Oneself and the Shrewdness of Sensuality

14. The other three precautions to be practiced in the wish to conquer one's own self and sensuality, the third enemy.

The first precaution

15. The first precaution is to understand that you have come to the monastery so that all may fashion you and try you. Thus, to free yourself from the imperfections and disturbances that can be engendered by the mannerisms and attitudes of the religious and draw profit from every occurrence, you should think that all in the community are artisans—as indeed they are—present there in order to prove you; that some will fashion you with words, others by deeds, and others with thoughts against you; and that in all this you must be submissive as is the statue to the craftsman who molds it, to the artist who paints it, and to the gilder who embellishes it.

If you fail to observe this precaution, you will not know how to overcome your sensuality and feelings, nor will you get along well in the community with the religious or attain holy peace or free yourself from many stumbling blocks and evils.

The second precaution

16. The second precaution is that you should never give up your works because of a want of satisfaction and delight in them, if they are fitting for the service of God. Neither should you carry out these works merely because of the satisfaction or delight they accord you, but you should do them just as you would the disagreeable ones. Otherwise it will be impossible for you to gain constancy and conquer your weakness.

The third precaution

17. The third precaution is that the interior person should never set eyes on the pleasant feelings found in spiritual exercises, becoming attached to them and carrying out these practices only for the sake of this satisfaction. Nor should such a person run from the bitterness that may be found in them, but rather seek the arduous and distasteful and embrace it. By this practice, sensuality is held in check; without this practice you will never lose self-love or gain the love of God.

Counsels to a Religious on How to Reach Perfection

Jesus Mariae filius

1. Your holy Charity with few words asked me for a great deal. An answer would require much time and paper. Seeing, then, that I lack both of these, I will try to be concise and jot down only certain points and counsels that in sum will contain much, so that whoever observes them perfectly will attain a high degree of perfection.

The one who wishes to be a true religious and fulfill the promises of the profession that was made to God, advance in virtue, and enjoy the consolations and the delight of the Holy Spirit, will be unable to do so without trying to practice with the greatest diligence the four following counsels concerning resignation, mortification, the practice of virtue, and bodily and spiritual solitude.

2. In order to practice the first counsel, concerning resignation, you should live in the monastery as though no one else were in it. And thus you should never, by word or by thought, meddle in things that happen in the community, nor with individuals in it, desiring not to notice their good or bad qualities or their conduct. And in order to preserve your tranquility of soul, even if the whole world crumbles you should not desire to advert to these things or interfere, remembering Lot's wife who was changed into hard stone because she turned her head to look at those who in the midst of much clamor and noise were perishing [Gn 19:26].

You should practice this with great fortitude, for you will thereby free yourself from many sins and imperfections and guard the tranquility and quietude of your soul with much profit before God and others.

Ponder this often, because it is so important that, for not observing it, many religious not only failed to improve through their other works of virtue and religious observance, but ever slipped back from bad to worse.

3. To practice the second counsel, which concerns mortification, and profit by it, you should engrave this truth on your heart. And it is that you have not come to the monastery for any other reason than to be worked and tried in virtue; you are like the stone that must be chiseled and fashioned before being set in the building.

Thus you should understand that those who are in the monastery are craftsmen placed there by God to mortify you by working and chiseling at you. Some will chisel with words, telling you what you would rather not hear; others by deed, doing against you what you would rather not endure; others by their temperament, being in their person and in their actions a bother and annoyance to you; and others by their thoughts, neither esteeming nor feeling love for you.

You ought to suffer these mortifications and annoyances with inner patience, being silent for love of God and understanding that you did not enter the religious life for any other reason than for others to work you in this way, and so you become worthy of heaven. If this was not your reason for entering the religious state, you should not have done so, but should have remained in the world to seek your comfort, honor, reputation, and ease.

4. The second counsel is wholly necessary for religious so they may fulfill the obligations of their state and find genuine humility, inward quietude, and joy in the Holy Spirit. If you do not practice this, you will know neither how to be a religious nor even why you came to the religious life. Neither will you know how to seek Christ (but only yourself), or find peace of soul, or avoid sinning and often feeling troubled.

Trials will never be lacking in religious life, nor does God want them to be. Since he brings souls there to be proved and purified, like gold, with hammer and the fire [Ecclus 2:5], it is fitting that they encounter trials and temptations from human beings and from devils, and the fire of anguish and affliction.

The religious must undergo these trials and should endeavor to bear them patiently and in conformity to God's will, and not so sustain them that instead of being approved by God in this affliction he be reproved for not having wanted to carry the cross of Christ in patience.

Since many religious do not understand that they have entered religious life to carry Christ's cross, they do not get along well with others. At the time of reckoning they will find themselves greatly confused and frustrated.

5. To practice the third counsel, which concerns the practice of virtue, you should be constant in your religious observance and in obedience without any concern for the world, but only for God. In order to achieve this and avoid being deceived, you should never set your eyes on the satisfaction or dissatisfaction of the work at hand as a motive for doing it or failing to do it, but on doing it for God. Thus you must undertake all things, agreeable or disagreeable, for the sole purpose of pleasing God through them.

6. To do this with fortitude and constancy and acquire the virtues quickly, you should take care always to be inclined to the difficult more than to the easy, to the rugged more than to the soft, to the hard and distasteful in a work more than to its delightful and pleasant aspects; and do not go about choosing what is less a cross, for the cross is a light burden [Mt 11:30]. The heavier a burden is, the lighter it becomes when borne for Christ.

You should try, too, by taking the lowest place always, that in things bringing comfort to your brothers in religion they be preferred to you. This you should do wholeheartedly, for it is the way to becoming greater in spiritual things, as God tells us in his Gospel:

Qui se humiliaverit exaltabitur ["Whoever humbles himself will be
exalted" (Mt 23:12)].

7. To practice the fourth counsel, which concerns solitude,
you should deem everything in the world as finished. Thus, when
(for not being able to avoid it) you have to deal with some matter,
do so in as detached a way as you would if it did not exist.

8. Pay no heed to the things out in the world, for God has already withdrawn and released you from them. Do not handle any
business yourself that you can do through a third person. It is very
fitting for you to desire to see no one and that no one see you.

And note carefully that if God will ask a strict account from all
the faithful of every idle word, how much more will he ask it of religious who have consecrated all their life and works to him. And God
will demand all of this on the day of reckoning.

9. I do not mean here that you fail to fulfill the duties of your
state with all necessary and possible care, and any others that obedience commands, but that you execute your tasks in such a way that
no fault is committed; for neither God nor obedience wants you to
commit a fault.

You should consequently strive to be incessant in prayer, and
in the midst of your corporal practices do not abandon it. Whether
you eat, or drink, or speak, or converse with lay people, or do anything else, you should always do so with desire for God and with your
heart fixed on him. This is very necessary for inner solitude, which
demands that the soul dismiss any thought that is not directed to
God. And in forgetfulness of all the things that are and happen in
this short and miserable life, do not desire to know anything in any
way except how better to serve God and keep the observance of your
institute.

10. If your Charity observes these four counsels with care, you
will reach perfection in a very short time. These counsels are so interdependent that if you are lacking in one of them, you will begin
to lose the profit and gain you have from practicing the others.

DEGREES OF PERFECTION

1. Do not commit a sin for all there is in the world, or any deliberate venial sin, or any known imperfection.

2. Endeavor to remain always in the presence of God, either real, imaginative, or unitive insofar as is permitted by your works.

3. Neither do anything nor say any notable word that Christ would not have done or said were he in the state I am, as old as I, and with the same kind of health.

4. Strive for the greater honor and glory of God in all things.

5. Do not omit mental prayer for any occupation, for it is the sustenance of your soul.

6. Do not omit examination of conscience because of any of your occupations, and for every fault do some penance.

7. Be deeply sorry for any time that is lost or that passes without your loving God.

8. In all things, both high and low, let God be your goal, for in no other way will you grow in merit and perfection.

9. Never give up prayer, and should you find dryness and difficulty, persevere in it for this very reason. God often desires to see what love your soul has, and love is not tried by ease and satisfaction.

10. In heaven and on earth, always the lowest and last place and office.

11. Never interfere in what you are not ordered to do, or be obstinate about anything, even though you may be right. And if, as

the saying goes, they give you an inch, do not take a mile. Some deceive themselves in such matters and think they have an obligation to do that which—if they reflect upon it well—in no way obliges them.

12. Pay no attention to the affairs of others, whether they be good or bad, for besides the danger of sin, this is a cause of distractions and lack of spirit.

13. Strive always to confess your sins with a deep knowledge of your own wretchedness and with clarity and purity.

14. Even though your obligations and duties are difficult and disagreeable to you, you should not become dismayed, for this will not always be so. And God, who proves the soul by a precept under the guise of a trial [Ps 94:20], will after a time accord it the experience of blessing and gain.

15. Remember always that everything that happens to you, whether prosperous or adverse, comes from God, so that you become neither puffed up in prosperity nor discouraged in adversity.

16. Remember always that you came here for no other reason than to be a saint; thus let nothing reign in your soul that does not lead you to sanctity.

17. Always be more disposed toward giving to others than giving to yourself, and thus you will not be envious of or selfish toward your neighbor. This is to be understood from the viewpoint of perfection, for God is angered with those who do not give precedence to his good pleasure over that of humans.

Soli Deo honor et gloria.

The Precautions of St. John of the Cross: Advice for the Spiritually Mature

The *Precautions* of St. John of the Cross are pithy warnings from a man who knows from experience that if one follows Christ to the end no burden is too great to bear. Though he directs his advice to Carmelite nuns, it is valuable for every Christian. Anyone who chooses to live the life of the spirit at a radical level can benefit from their reading.

Be detached, be patient, be careful are repeated counsels in St. John's vocabulary. It takes time to become spiritually mature. There are many pitfalls to overcome with the help of grace. We meet one or another enemy at every turn of the road. The life of the spirit entails trial and error. The ways of God are not our ways.

From the start the saint cautions us to go slowly, according to God's timetable, if we want to reach the goal set by grace:

> 1. The soul must practice the following instructions if it wishes to attain in a short time holy recollection and spiritual silence, nakedness, and poverty of spirit, where one enjoys the peaceful comfort of the Holy Spirit, reaches union with God, is freed of all the obstacles incurred from the creatures of this world, defended against the wiles and deceits of the devil, and liberated from one's own self.

That for which we strive—quiet, candor, humility—direct us to three equally important signs of spiritual maturity. The first of these is "the peaceful comfort of the Holy Spirit." The second is "union with God." The third is freedom from three formidable obstacles: from the world in its worldliness; from the devil, the master of malice and deceit; and from our own selfish sensuality.

Let us consider what it feels like to enjoy comfort in a human sense. Then we can appreciate how much more comforting must be the peaceful presence of the Holy Spirit.

It is a hot July day. I am working in my grandmother's garden. It is time to tie the bean shoots to poles. The number of plants seems infinite, but I tie them all. That job done, I decide to hoe the dirt around the corn. The earth is hard, sun-parched, so it takes more effort on my part to dig. My shirt is soaked with perspiration.

Though the garden is a lot of work, it's my grandmother's pride and joy. I continue working, trying not to think about how tired and thirsty I am. Footsteps! I turn and see her standing there with a pitcher of cool lemonade and a frosty glass. I give her a hug. We walk to the edge of the garden. I take the glass she offers with a knowing smile and drink, slowly at first, then with deeper gulps. I savor the last few mouthfuls, greatly refreshed.

I go back in time and memory to graduate school days. For months I have been studying for comprehensive exams. I feel exhausted. My mind is like a stuffed sausage. I am unable to absorb any more ideas. I long for a breath of fresh air I get up from my study table and go out for a walk. The river is not far away from where I live. Like a desert nomad in need of an oasis, I walk briskly to the water's edge and sit down. At first my mind will not stay still. I wait and watch the rippling waves. The sun is warm. Coal barges float by. A boy fishes with his dad. A twig drifts into view. My head clears. I am able to think.

As lovely as these occasions of body-mind refreshment may be, "the peaceful comfort of the Holy Spirit" is infinitely more consoling. This is a peace the world cannot give (cf. Jn 14:27), a level of peace I cannot control at will. Such spirit-inspired refreshment is a pure gift. We cannot demand it; we can only ready ourselves to receive it by creating the conducive conditions of "holy recollection, silence, nakedness, and poverty of spirit."

In other words, we have to overcome distractions, seek inner and outer stillness, hide nothing from God, and operate, as St. John would say, from the center of our humility.

In this peaceful refreshment, the soul attains the rest in God it seeks, however many obstacles block its path. Countless are the seductive ways of the world, the wiles of the devil, the futile attempts we make to put the pride form, not the Christ form, at the center of our life. Yet the soul in search of spiritual maturity seeks the freedom to pursue its goal of oneness with God in as short a time as possible. This is the fruit of "naked" faith, undying hope, and selfless love.

To ready ourselves for the grace of transforming union, if and when God grants us this gift, we must follow the path of the *Precautions*. The instructions we receive will free us from the deceptive ties that bind us to the created in forgetfulness of our Creator. Only when we let go of inordinate attachments to people, events, and things as ultimate can we free ourselves for lasting attachment to God. Detachment is not a negative act. It is a positive commitment to distance ourselves from what is passing so as to bind ourselves to the eternal, to what is lasting.

We are to free ourselves not only from the hindrances of the world and "the wiles and deceits of the devil" but also from our own self. What does this mean?

Once as a child I took some expensive perfume from my aunt's dresser, thinking it would never be missed. I was wrong. Since I had used what I took to play "make-believe," it was too late to make restitution, and I was too embarrassed to confess. For many days I felt weighed down by guilt. How could I have done such a thing? I had never stolen anything. All this self-questioning only served to increase the burden of sin. At last I decided to admit to the deed and ask forgiveness. I went to my aunt and told her the truth. It was I who had taken the perfume she wanted to wear last week. To my happy surprise she had forgotten the incident. She thanked me for trusting her enough to confess. She forgave me. My guilt lifted. I felt lighthearted.

This was for me an experience of being "liberated" from a part of myself that had become burdensome to me. Is there a lesson in this incident that can help us to understand what St. John means by promising us liberation from our own self?

The side of us that hinders spiritual growth is not our deepest self formed in Christ, but the side that wants to manage the world. Making our seemingly self-sufficient ego ultimate is the third obstacle from which we must disencumber ourselves if we want to experience the peace and comfort of a Christ-centered life.

Through recollection, silence, and the practice of inner poverty, the ways of the Lord should become so habitual that every action is an expression of love. We imitate Christ with such habitual care that selfishness lessens its power over us.

An implied caution seems to be that we ought not to make extraordinary efforts to live the life of holiness, for then we might concentrate more on the self and its progress than on God. We must strive instead to live spiritually within our routine day-to-day existence. The danger of attempting to seek the Spirit by extraordinary means may lead us into making these means ends in themselves. In ordinary things like cooking a meal and caring for children, walking to work and participating in a parish, Jesus has to be found.

By remaining open to God's presence in and behind every ordinary appearance, we will reach perfection before we know it. Such perfection is a byproduct of dying to the old self and finding new life in Christ. In other words, we have to stop "Easing God Out," a definition of "EGO" that seems accurate.

According to the instructions St. John will now impart, the obstacle least difficult (though, especially in our consumer era, not easy) to conquer is the world.

The enemy hardest to understand—as dense as the mystery of iniquity itself—is the Prince of Darkness, the devil. The hindrance that has the fastest hold on us is, not surprisingly, the "flesh" or that part of us that is unspiritualized, that resists the forming, reforming, and transforming power of grace, that would choose irresponsible unintegrated sexuality over other-centered integrated spirituality. Realist as he is, St. John says of selfish sensuality, "its attacks continue as long as the old self lasts."

Before naming and analyzing these stumbling blocks to spiritual maturity in detail, the saint articulates the goal of the *Precautions:*

3. To gain complete mastery over any of these three enemies, one must vanquish all three of them; and in the weakening of one, the other two are weakened also. When all three are over-powered, no further war remains for the soul.

What are the conditions St. John proposes if we want to profit fully from this sound advice? In many of his writings, and here, too, in the *Precautions,* St. John follows the way of paradox.

> To reach satisfaction in all
> desire satisfaction in nothing.
> To come to possess all
> desire the possession of nothing.
> To arrive at being all
> desire to be nothing.[1]

If God is to be our all in All, then anything less than God must be annihilated as an ultimate concern. To follow one wish list after another can be unnerving. No sooner is one desire fulfilled than another presents itself. Desires by this definition can never be satisfied. Thus a necessary condition to facilitate maturity of spirit is the banishment of uncontrolled appetites or desires. Any inordinate attachment breeds agitation, restlessness, and lack of inner peace. By contrast, the fruits of the spirit are liberation, prudence, contemplation, and charity.

Our Three Enemies and Their Overpowering

What makes the world the least difficult enemy to conquer? Life in the world is not that simple. No matter how much we want to practice detachment, the demands of the day catch us unaware. Before we know it, we are victims of the consumer mentality. What St. John says helps us to place the world in its proper perspective.

The moment we reflect upon the essential temporality of our existence, the world ceases to be so formidable an enemy. We are no longer bound to the spirit of materialism. We can love the world and use its gifts, knowing all the while that material goods cannot satisfy us wholly. Everything that promises fulfillment passes away.

Only one thing does not pass away, the spirit of the Lord. He tells us that his kingdom is not of this world (cf. Jn 18:36). We who follow him must be in this world, not of it. In him alone, do we find peace:

> I have told you this
> so that you might have peace in me.
> In the world you will have trouble,
> but take courage,
> I have conquered the world. (Jn 16:33, NAB)

The world holds no lasting fascination when we live in it in conformity to Christ. We see ourselves as stewards of a divine gift, not as conquerors or predators. Christ himself shows us the secret of overcoming the world in its worldliness when he goes into the desert for forty days and forty nights (cf. Lk 4:1-13). There he is tempted by all that the world has to offer—power, pleasure, and possession—if only he will betray his mission from the Father. Because Christ chooses to be obedient to his call, the devil has no power over him.

Still, as St. John says, "The devil is the hardest to understand." The difficulty he senses seems to be related to the inner torment described by St. Paul:

> For I know that good does not dwell in me, that is, in my flesh. The willing is ready at hand, but doing the good is not. For I do not do the good I want, but I do the evil I do not want. (Rom 7:18-19, NAB)

The power of evil perverts the good. The demonic is present under a thousand disguises. Evil is difficult to discern. False "gods" may be erected before we recognize them. In our age, technology may become the only "god" we obey. Outwardly the quest for power may triumph over human concern. Inwardly the demonic may take the form of envy, jealousy, deceit.

And what of the flesh? St. John says it "is the most tenacious, and its attacks continue as long as the old self lasts." The "old self" is surely the part of us that hears the word but fails to heed it. We are victims of the flesh not merely in a sexual sense but in terms of such sensual satisfactions as pride, anger, agitation, gluttony, and greed. These passions tear us apart. Peace is impossible when a person lies and cheats while playing the pious professional, when he or she clings to wealth at the expense of the poor, as if coffers piled high will guarantee a place in heaven.

The miracle is that we have been redeemed through grace, that God so loved the world that he found us worthy to receive everlasting life (cf. Jn 3:16). The more Christ-like we become, the better are our chances to overpower these three enemies—to put off the old self and put on the new, to leave fears behind and leap into the darkness of faith to such a degree that "no further war remains for the soul."

Overview of Our Three Enemies

Enemy Number One: The World

The world is too much with me. Morning dawns. Light banishes the sweetness of sleep, and the world rushes in upon me. Is my first thought to ask God to bless this day? Hardly! I flick on the radio for the weather report. The war, a local fire, the five-day forecast, and the world rushes in upon me.

I feel thirsty. I feel hungry. Is my first thought to thank God for a refrigerator full of food? Not really. I pull open the door, down some juice, make toast and coffee. And the world rushes in upon me.

My day. In my mind I schedule the appointments that will occupy the morning hours. No time for a leisurely lunch. Rush! There is a rescheduled committee meeting I must attend. I have an hour or so to prepare my report. Rush! I should have typed it the night before. I have to be subtle, diplomatic when it's my turn to present. Hurry now! I finish dressing, slam the front door, run down the steps, jump into the car, turn on the ignition. Nothing. The engine won't start. Be calm. It's cold. Turn the key again. Ignition. I'm off. The stop light is turning yellow. Why wait for the red? I gun the engine. Made it! I drive on, down the hillside, across the bridge.

Minor traffic jam. I move into the other lane and give the car some gas. Up one hill, down the next. Good! My favorite parking place is free. I swing in and shut off the motor. Find my office keys, unlock the door, hang up my coat, look at the clock. Just on time!

In all these ways, I make the world my enemy. In its "worldliness" it rushes in upon me. It fills every minute of my life with worldly concerns. I forget that with each tick of the clock I am closer to eternity. My attitude has to change. The world only becomes my enemy when I allow it to alienate me from my Divine Source. Then the temporal makes me unmindful of the eternal.

I am beginning to understand St. John's caution against the world. The world in itself is not my enemy. I make it my enemy when my attitude toward it isolates me from the eternal. Cautioned by St. John, I may catch myself before it is too late. Then my day will be the same, but there will be a noticeable change in my attitude toward it.

Morning dawns. I awaken slowly and take an extra moment to say thanks for the gift of this day. I eat and feel grateful for the food on my table. While dressing, I try to center my thoughts on the Lord. "Even if I do not think of you explicitly, Lord, let me do what I do for your sake."

While watching my driving, I take a few moments for recollection. I stop at the traffic light and look out over hills, knowing that his presence is everywhere. I intersperse mental plans for my morning with brief meditations on God's providential care. In this way I save myself a lot of needless aggravation over a day that will work itself out anyway.

By the time I arrive at the office , my working day has already taken on a deeper meaning. What might have been a merely functional approach is replaced by a rhythmic blend of contemplation and action, leisure and labor—all because of a shift in attitude.

Whether preparing reports or chairing meetings, my whole demeanor will be more calm and collected if my time is grounded in the eternal. I realize that I can be patient. Life is a gradual unfolding. What I do not accomplish today, I can do tomorrow. My time becomes more God's time. In God's good time, tensions are resolved.

In this way, the world, instead of being my enemy, becomes my friend. Instead of keeping me a prisoner cut off from God, it becomes a path that leads me closer to the eternal reaches of time.

Enemy Number Two: The Devil

To make us forget our dependence on God is the devil's desire. The Evil One plays on our pride. The Prince of Deceit tempts us to think we can save ourselves. He tricks us into believing that nothing can stand in the way of "my will."

A friend of mine completed her degree in social work. She was understandably proud of the good grades she received and the job offer she accepted in a government office in the ghetto section of the city. She was armed with knowledge from books but little life experience. Suddenly she was up against evil in every form. It was nothing to lie, cheat, and steal, to pit race against race, for no apparent reason. Techniques that worked so well in school failed to work here. People whom she thought would be receptive to her help only took advantage of her. They played on her good will while looking out for their gain. Some seemed to understand the love in her heart, but others turned away. The possibility of failure made her doubly determined to redeem the ignorant from their lack of understanding. She would show them how to overcome hatred and hypocrisy. She would teach them how to trust.

Her good will was thus tainted by willfulness. It was only after she had failed time and again that she began to see that it was not the people who were her enemies but herself. Once she realized how twisted her motives had become, she was able to avoid the "devilish" snare of the "savior complex." Her experiences renewed her sense of dependence on God while weakening the false pride of total self-reliance. She began to delve into her motives. She sensed when dreams of success masqueraded as humble desires to serve, when pride posed as pity, when the need for praise slipped in under the cover of compassion. For her to admit to failure was not easy, but this admission marked a new start. The devil is not so formidable an adversary when we acknowledge our own sinfulness before God and our need for redemption.

Enemy Number Three: My "Self"

The enmity posed by the old self is more subtle than lust. We are upset by anger, envy, and jealousy, by hostility, anxiety, and depression. Anger, to use this example, is a "fleshy" phenomenon. Its effects can be felt by us long after the initial trigger has disappeared.

Elaine was the eldest in a family of two other sisters. Around the age of fifteen, she began to notice what she had tried not to see before: her parents seemed to favor her younger sister. Several instances convinced her that this favoritism was not a matter of her imagination. True, Betsy was brighter than she, a more talented girl in some areas, and quite pretty. When both of the girls brought good grades home, everyone fussed over Betsy. Elaine was angry at her parents, but she tried not to show it. When she did express her feelings, she was reprimanded, so she seethed in silence.

Years went by. She and her sister drifted apart. Both of them led successful lives. There was nothing to be angry or envious about anymore, especially after their parents died. Elaine had long since made her peace with them, but something still prevented the girls from being close. When her sister was around, Elaine felt the old anger welling up, not just emotionally but bodily. She realized that she had never really forgiven her. She knew what was wrong, but she did not want to make the first move toward a resolution of her feelings of animosity and unfairness.

Anger is tenacious. Just as the world and the devil may isolate us from God, so too selfishness in the form of anger and hostility separates us from the mercy and forgiveness of Jesus. Yet our hope resides in St. John of the Cross's promise that if we weaken one of these enemies, all three will be weakened in turn. The way to the peace Christ promises us will open. Even if the three enemies are not overcome entirely, any effort we make in this direction reminds us to rely on the Lord and to trust in the grace of his redemption.

Following this general reflection, we can look specifically at each *Precaution,* beginning with what St. John says about the world.

The First Precaution Against the World

"To free yourself from the harm the world can do you, you should practice three precautions."

The words of the first precaution are characteristically deep. They invite us to a thoughtful reading in which we try as much as possible to "bracket" our spontaneous prejudices as well as our hopes for an "instant technique" for spiritual perfection. What St. John provides is a way to ready ourselves for the gift of contemplative union, should God grant this to us. He makes no guarantee. His appeal is not to our will power but to our poverty of spirit. We need all the grace God can give if we are to commit ourselves in faith and dedication to following Christ.

St. John appeals to that in us which wants to be an instrument of God's will. He challenges us to live *in* this world without being *of* this world. In the words of the first precaution, he invites us to a new way of loving:

5. The first is that you should have an equal love for and an equal forgetfulness of all persons, whether relatives or not, and withdraw your heart from relatives as much as from others, and in some ways even more for fear that flesh and blood might be quickened by the natural love that is ever alive among kin, and must always be mortified for the sake of spiritual perfection.

6. Regard all as strangers, and you will fulfill your duty toward them better than by giving them the affection you owe God. Do not love one person more than another, for you will err; the person who loves God more is the one more worthy of love, and you do not know who this is. But forgetting everyone alike, as is necessary for holy recollection, you will free yourself from this error of loving one person more or less than another.

Do not think about others, neither good things nor bad. Flee them inasmuch as possible. And if you do not observe this practice, you will not know how to be a religious, nor will you be able to reach holy recollection or deliver yourself from imperfections. And if you should wish to allow yourself some freedom in this matter, the devil will deceive you in one way or another, or you will deceive yourself under some guise of good or evil.

> In doing what we said, you will have security, for in no other
> way will you be capable of freeing yourself from the imperfec-
> tions and harm derived from creatures.

What might this first precaution imply for those of us who wish
at the same time to love and serve the world, as Christ loved and served
it, and yet who also want to join with Christ in his condemnation of
the world? In other words, how is it possible to live at once in the
world with equal love and equal forgetfulness?

Consider this example. Larry had gone from being a common
laborer to becoming the executive director and owner of his own
business. He was married, had five lovely daughters, and was making more money than he ever dreamed possible when he was "just a
railroad man." Lately he had begun to ask himself some serious
questions.

"I have so much," he thought. "A beautiful home and kids in
good schools, two cars in the garage, a great wife with whom I can
travel when I want. I have plenty of money put away for retirement,
and yet I'm a nervous wreck. My stomach is upset. My gall bladder is
killing me. A few weeks ago I went to the doctor and got a bill for
two hundred dollars, and I don't know what he did! He told me to
go home and relax. It was just my nerves. Just my nerves! Tonight
for the first time in two weeks at a small faith-sharing group I found
a little peace. I wish I could stay this calm, but I know what will happen. Tomorrow I'll be in my car caught in traffic. My stomach will
knot up. I can't relax. When I get home, I don't dare take a drink.
My stomach is so bad I tell my wife I don't want anything to eat.
Maybe I'll eat later but in the meantime dinner is spoiled. What's
the use of talking? Maybe I need to see a shrink. Maybe he can tell
me what's the matter with me. Why can't I find some meaning in
life?"

One reason might be that Larry is trying so hard to live up to
external expectations that he has neglected to find his real self. Now
that hidden self is crying out to be heard. He remarked that he had
once been a practicing Catholic but had given up on religion long
ago under the pressure of the world. Since his practice of the faith
was only perfunctory, it was easily replaced by other more practical
concerns. The trouble was that these concerns had not brought him

peace. He now wondered what they were all about. Perhaps this very wondering marks the beginning of a change for the better.

Larry' s life reveals an imbalance regarding the question of equal love and equal forgetfulness. He catered to the world so much that he forgot the necessity of opposing its demands. He stressed involvement to the point of excluding any kind of detachment. Thus in this first precaution, St. John reminds us of a fundamental rhythm of the spiritual life: between involvement and detachment, being wholly present where we are and at the same time not making of our presence there an ultimate concern.

Something similar can be said of our care for relatives and friends. No matter how deep it is, it can never replace the one thing needful: union with God in love for the sake of serving him in this world. To be free for this task, we must overcome any exclusive attachment we feel for relatives and friends. This is the string that ties us down and prevents us from loving everyone in the Lord. Christ says the same:

> Whoever loves father or mother more than me is not worthy of me, and whoever loves son or daughter more me is not worthy of me; whoever does not take up his cross and follow after me is not worthy of me. Whoever finds his life will lose it, and whoever loses his life for my sake will find it. (Mt 10:37-39, NAB)

When we treat others as we would "strangers"—loving them equally but not giving them the affection owed only to God—we loosen ourselves from the obstacles of over-dependence and over-attachment. We foster affective independence or forgetfulness of the narcissistic emotional ties that prevent pure love.

St. John of the Cross is not saying that we are to cease caring for our relatives or for those in need; he simply wants us to keep the proper perspective. True Christian love strives to love the other in Christ. He is the source of all human love, the exemplar of the ways by which we express this love concretely in our lives.

By making God the center of our love, rather than any created person or thing, we guard against loving others in an overly dependent way. We are less likely to make relationships ends in themselves. If this happens, we need to correct our course by *forgetting* our inordinate bonds to the other and *remembering* that God is the ground of our love.

Love and forgetfulness are like two evenly weighted scales; they keep us balanced at the center. We do not grant to any one person the affection we owe God alone. At the same time, we are aware that our love for God must manifest itself in the care we show for others. Human love will then be an outflow of the love we reserve for God alone.

Christian love is always directed by our capacity for self-giving in the situation where we happen to be. The fact that our expression of love is limited reminds us that we can do only so much. There are some situations about which we can do nothing. Here especially we must learn to care with equal love and equal forgetfulness.

If we are to incarnate Christ's love in the world, we must extend it equally to all. At the same time, we must be careful not to confuse love with the degree of aid or assistance we can give. A nurse may spend three hours with one patient and five minutes with another. The degree of love in both cases may be equal though circumstances dictate that the kind of nursing aid each patient receives will be different.

In the same quotation, St. John says that we are to hold those we love, relatives or not, as strangers to us. In this way we will serve them better than by "giving them the affection" we owe to God alone.

In other words, between ourselves and those we love there has to be a relation of caring and not caring. While equally loving them all, we must be equally detached from them, for equal love can only be understood in the light of equal forgetfulness. Forgetfulness requires that we give the fullness of our affection and attachment to God alone. We must hold the ones we love at a certain distance from us, lest we forget that we are in the last analysis strangers to one another, known in the fullest sense only to God.

To look upon the other as in some essential way a stranger is to look upon him or her as unique. We must respect the mystery others are and not attach ultimate affection to them. We owe such affection only to God. Love for God liberates us to love others as they really are. For it is only God who knows us as we are, and it is only in

God that we are able to love others without making undue demands upon them.

All people are worthy, therefore, of our love, but no person is worthy of *all* of it. The fullness of love finds its beginning and its end in God.

> Do not love one person more than another, for you will err; the person who loves God more is the one more worthy of love, and you do not know who this is.

We do not know who it is that God deems most worthy of our love. God may love a person more who in our eyes appears to be a great sinner. An alcoholic who neglects his family, for example, may in his heart not wish to hurt them, but perhaps cannot help himself. God understands his good intention and loves him in spite of his weakness. But we cannot see him as God does. From a practical viewpoint, he seems incompetent to us. While we may not entrust him with a position of great responsibility, we cannot pass final judgment on him. That right belongs to God alone.

> But forgetting everyone alike, as is necessary for holy recollection, you will free yourself from this error of loving one person more or less than another.

If we are inordinately attached to no one but God, we can move more quickly into recollection. We let others fade momentarily into the background as we bring ourselves before the Lord. We are not inclined to show more affection for one person than for another. We have equal love for all because we are equally forgetful of all. Thus we keep ourselves from falling into error regarding the degree of love we owe to each.

As our love becomes more pure, we cease concentrating on the good or bad qualities people possess. Of such matters, St. John says, "Do not think about others, neither good things nor bad. Flee them inasmuch as possible." Any kind of preoccupation with what others do makes it impossible for us to be with God in holy recollection.

Regarding this style of living in equal love and equal forgetfulness, John cautions that the devil will be on the lookout to deceive us. The world, too, will try to seduce us to seek unbounded love of its pleasures and possessions. We will pay a terrible price if we lose our balance. Life itself may lose its meaning.

By comparison, to live in equal love and equal forgetfulness brings with it a special reward: "In doing what we said, you will have security." St. John does not mean the kind of security that comes with a pension or a life insurance policy. The security he means could be compared with the security of a tree when its roots trail deeply below the surface of the soil. In the same way we will be secure when our roots plunge into the *terra firma* of our loving surrender to God. In this person-to-Person relationship of love lies lasting security. In and through it, we disentangle ourselves from any attachment that may displace our lasting attachment to the Eternal.

The Second Precaution Against the World

7. The second precaution against the world concerns temporal goods. To free yourself truly of the harm stemming from this kind of good and to moderate the excess of your appetite, you should abhor all manner of possessions and not allow yourself to worry about these goods, neither for food, nor for clothing, nor for any other created thing, nor for tomorrow, and direct this care to something higher—to seeking the kingdom of God (seeking not to fail God); and the rest, as His Majesty says, will be added unto us [Mt 6:33], for he who looks after the beasts will not be forgetful of you. By this practice you will attain silence and peace in the senses.

Temporal goods, if we are to experience their real goodness, must not be seen apart from their Giver. They are not ends in themselves but epiphanic manifestations. The beauty of the eternal shines through every temporal thing. All creation participates in the goodness of God, who holds each one in being. Anything idolized in isolation from its Divine Source becomes a source of greedy possessiveness and useless worry about what we do or do not have.

St. John gives this precaution to nuns with a solemn vow of poverty, for whom personal ownership of goods was not an issue (or so it would seem). They were to abhor all manner of possessions so as to direct their care "to something higher." Nonexcessive care for worldly goods freed the sisters to enjoy God's gifts while letting go of anything that might displace their love for God. Can we who live in the world do likewise? Can we care for material goods without becoming totally absorbed in them?

Such a precaution may grate on ears accustomed to mass advertising. The media beckon us to buy our way to happiness. A commercial society would never warn us of the danger of "excess of appetite." The more we have, the more we want; the more we want, the more we get. The day may come when we discover that we are possessed by our possessions.

To measure the value of life on the basis of what we own is the cause of many a sleepless night. Clutching on to things, we forget their temporality. Care for them overwhelms care for our inner life. We grow careless about what matters most.

What we are to "abhor" are not the necessities of life, like food, clothing, and shelter. To be avoided is lasting attachment to any of these things. When we see things becoming the beginning and end of our concern, it is time to take this precaution seriously. We must detach ourselves from any thing, situation, or person to prevent it from becoming so primary that we forget the primacy of our relationship to the Lord. Remember what he said about the lilies of the field and the birds of the air:

> Look at the birds in the sky; they do not sow or reap, they gather nothing into barns, yet your heavenly Father feeds them. Are you not more important than they? ...Learn from the way wild flowers grow. They do not work or spin. But I tell you that not even Solomon in all his splendor was clothed like one of them. If God so clothes the grass of the field...will he not much more provide for you...? (Mt 6:26-30, NAB).

It is not easy to be this trusting, to believe that God cares for us personally. It is especially not easy to trust in the Lord when our desires are not fulfilled, when what we need is not forthcoming. Our inclination is to worry excessively about the morrow. Sensible planning is fine. We have to gather the harvest into barns, but our tendency is to go overboard, saying we trust in God and at the same time acting as if created things will insure our happiness. We want to organize our life in such a way that our future is secure. We act as if we have to control the world when really we have nothing to say about it.

Complete trust in God is hard to come by in this age. We are more prone to trust ourselves and to relinquish trust in God. Yet the same age that tempts us to rely on material things to save us is the testing ground for faith. The more the world in its worldliness beckons us to forget God, the more we are confronted by the fact of our finitude.

The most materially affluent society may be the poorest spiritually. Possessiveness appears foolish once we direct our concerns to a higher plane. Products famous a few months ago are now off the shelf. Things that promised to make us happy are in the trash. Nothing finite can fulfill us spiritually. We thank God for every good gift, but we make none of them ultimate. We know that only God's word does not pass away (cf. Mt 24:34-35, NAB).

The impermanence of our throw-away culture teaches us that all else is secondary to union with God. The Lord is there when we need him most. He hears the cry of the poor. He gives us the comfort we seek. The world strews countless obstacles on our path, but Christ brushes them away, "for he who looks after the beasts will not be forgetful of you."

"By this practice," says St. John of the Cross, "you will attain silence and peace in the senses." More often than not such inner quiet eludes us. Our eyes dart from one desired object to the next. Our hands grasp when they should give. Our restless hearts do not rest in God. We long for the peace and silence John promises as the fruit of the practice of Christ-centered detachment. We know that Christ's promise of peace (cf. Jn 16:33) is the best protection we can find against the excess of appetite that prevents us from seeking God.

The Spirit works in such mysterious ways that we may attain peace when we least expect it, or feel least deserving of it. Detachment readies us to receive this gift, for only when we open our hearts to God by stilling gnawing fears associated with gaining and losing do we sense what Jesus meant when he said "I have conquered the world" (Jn 16:33).

The Third Precaution Against the World

Words do not necessarily reveal what is in a person's heart. Chatter may betray a lack of inwardness. Some words may only fill up the silence. others may replace charity and compassion with cynicism and spite. Words may heal or wound.

The ideal proposed in this third precaution against the world is to use words in such a way that they express our love and respect. Idle gossip, meddling in others' business, cutting envy, or subtle seduction belie the message John of the Cross wants to convey:

> 8. The third precaution is very necessary so you may know how to guard yourself in the community against all harm that may arise in regard to the religious. Many, by not observing it, not only have lost the peace and good of their souls but have fallen and ordinarily continue to fall into many evils and sins.
>
> It is that you very carefully guard yourself against thinking about what happens in the community, and even more against speaking of it, of anything in the past or present concerning a particular religious: nothing about his or her character or conduct or deeds no matter how serious any of this seems. Do not say anything under the color of zeal or of correcting a wrong, unless at the proper time to whomever by right you ought to tell. Never be scandalized or astonished at anything you happen to see or learn of, endeavoring to preserve your soul in forgetfulness of all that.

The meaning of this precaution extends beyond the enclosure; it invites us to consider some universal implications of communication and community.

To guard ourselves against evil in interrelationships implies guarding our intentions. We ought to will the good of the other in accordance with the command of Christ. Though we may fail at times to live up to the ideal of chaste, respectful love, we are obliged to try. Such obstacles as the penchant for disrespect or indulgence in empty gossip at the expense of another's reputation must be shunned.

An old but true adage is that "the road to hell is paved with good intentions." We have to discern if what we say of a person is

good only in our own eyes, or if we are behaving in the way Christ
would:

> Many, by not observing it [this precaution], not only have lost
> the peace and good of their souls but have fallen and ordinarily
> continue to fall into many evils and sins.

To follow the way of Christian communication exemplified by
Jesus, we ought to begin by listening to what the Lord is saying in
our personal life here and now. Then, out of this solitary listening,
we can try to communicate his word to others. What inspires people
is not so much the words we speak but the way we are when we speak
them.

"Carefully guard yourself against thinking about what happens
in the community, and even more against speaking of it." St. John
admonishes persons who are overly preoccupied with what others
are doing instead of quietly living their lives in union with God. Instead of examining their own consciences, they are only too ready
to criticize others. Rather than correcting their own faults, they are
intent upon rectifying the misdeeds of the people around them.

Not only must we keep our minds uncluttered by such concerns; we must also cease speaking of them. Our seeming concern
for others may be in reality a betrayal of charity. Endless chatter does
not represent an overflow of love for the other or for God. What
matters to us is to satisfy our curiosity or to air our anger, jealousy,
and hurt pride. John of the Cross does not mince words in criticiz-
ing such sickly curiosity: "[Say] nothing about his or her character
or conduct or deeds no matter how serious any of this seems."

What is a person's character? It is more than the public image
others have of us. It signifies the formation of our heart. Sometimes
this image is like the person we are, but this is not always the case.
No outsider knows us in our inmost self as God does. How then can
another judge my character in an ultimate sense? This is impossible.

St. John of the Cross says, therefore, that it is best not to speak
publicly of another's character. Privately I may feel as if there are
some discrepancies in your behavior. I can reflect on these in silence
or at most in confidence with a trusted friend. To make your character an object of public surveillance, to make a judgment on your

reputation that may not accord at all with the person you are, is unacceptable in a Christian community.

Nor may I speak of your manner of life. It may well be that it offends my own standards. Your way of doing things may not be in agreement with my ideal of what should be done. Still, the respect I have for you as a person must go deeper than my preferences about the way you live or the lifestyle you exemplify.

Generally it is best, as St. John says, not to speak of a person's manner of life, of his or her character or business. This kind of speaking more often than not degenerates into unfounded gossip. It is best to guard our tongue and to leave such appraisal to the discretion of whomever in the community is delegated with authority.

We need to be cautioned in this regard, for all of us tend to speak too easily about others "under the color of zeal or of correcting a wrong." The do-gooder in us does not necessarily have the other's best interest at heart.

John of the Cross adds that we are not to speak of these things among one another. However, if we are convinced in conscience that someone else's manner of life seriously endangers the community, we can communicate our concern to those to whom it is right to speak "at the proper time." Such a respectful approach to problematic people is more Christian than the usual gossipy way we handle difficult situations. Nothing is more terrible than to ruin another's reputation without having real evidence at hand. All we draw upon is the false accusation of our assumptions.

Christian communication implies prayerful surrender to the word of God speaking in ourselves and others. Out of this respectful openness there emerges the wisdom to know when to speak and when to be silent. When we do have to say something, we do so wisely and moderately, and to the appropriate person. In persistently trying to see the other against the background of the Sacred, we preserve inner peace. In such a climate, we are less likely to be "scandalized" or "astonished" at anything we happen to hear. We become rather shockproof. Instead of dramatizing every event out of proportion, we strive "to preserve [our] soul in forgetfulness of all that."

Forgetfulness does not mean indifference or lack of concern. It is instead the mark of persons who are willing to be silent about another's mistakes, who refuse to call attention to themselves by telling an enticing story at another's expense. What we try to forget are the superficial diagnoses made by idle gossipers, the innuendos of people consumed by curiosity, the excuses they use to belittle others. We try as well to forget our bruised pride, the times we've been jealous, the irritation and antipathy we've felt.

Christian forgetfulness is the willingness to turn the other cheek when someone we trusted betrays us. It means seeing behind nasty remarks the loneliness of a man without friends, behind envy a woman who has lost self-respect, behind violence an adolescent deprived of genuine love.

Only when we listen can we truly speak. Listening to the voice of the Spirit who speaks within us prompts us not to engage in idle gossip. It allows us to address others out of respect for their integrity.

Such speaking and listening are the core of Christian communication. St. John displays his knowledge of this art and discipline when he describes relations with people.

> 9. For, should you desire to pay heed to things, many will seem wrong, even were you to live among angels, because of your not understanding the substance of them. Take Lot's wife as an example: Because she was troubled at the destruction of the Sodomites and turned her head to watch what was happening, God punished her by converting her into a pillar of salt [Gn 19:26]. You are thus to understand God's will: that even were you to live among devils you should not turn the head of your thoughts to their affairs, but forget these things entirely and strive to keep your soul occupied purely and entirely in God, and not let the thought of this thing or that hinder you from so doing.
>
> And to achieve this, be convinced that in monasteries and communities there is never a lack of stumbling blocks, since there is never a lack of devils who seek to overthrow the saints; God permits this in order to prove and try religious.
>
> And if you do not guard yourself, acting as though you were not in the house, you will not know how to be a religious no matter how much you do, nor will you attain holy denudation and recollection or free yourself of the harm arising from these

things. If you are not cautious in this manner, no matter how good your intention and zeal, the devil will catch you in one way or another. And you are already fully captive when you allow yourself distractions of this sort.

Recall what the Apostle St. James asserts: If anyone thinks he is religious, not restraining the tongue, that one's religion is vain [Jas 1:26]. This applies as much to the interior as to the exterior tongue.

What we find in this text are laws and dynamics fundamental to a mature spiritual life. St. John says, in effect, that if we consider what happens in community, saying things under the pretext of zeal or out of a genuine desire to help, then we will find something wrong even if we "live among angels."

This remark emphasizes how often we conclude that something is amiss because we lack the proper understanding of what is being done or said. The same happens when we are in too much of a hurry to consider the spiritual knowledge and advice a master like St. John is imparting. We thus come to a faulty judgment.

John asks us to consider what happened to Lot's wife. "Because she was troubled at the destruction of the Sodomites and turned her head to watch what was happening, God punished her by converting her into a pillar of salt." Lot's wife was more intent on satisfying her curiosity than on following God's command. She should have been forgetful of the past, focusing only on obeying the will of God.

Similarly, St. John tells the sisters that even if they live among devils, they should "strive to keep [their] soul occupied purely and entirely in God, and not let the thought of this thing or that hinder [them] from so doing."

St. John seems to say that it is better to keep our thoughts centered on God's will for us here and now than to be unduly perturbed by what we have or have not done in the past. Especially if we have confessed our faults and received absolution, it is unwise to review them scrupulously.

Likewise we must not busy ourselves with the business of others. We need to live a more recollected life, undistracted by "this or that." Binding ourselves to God's will makes it easier to retain inner equanimity in the midst of business dealings and inevitable bickering. This kind of centered presence allows all dimensions of life to fall into their proper place in the light of God's allowing and inviting will.

In the understanding he has of human nature, St. John admits that no community will be without some occasion for stumbling. Inner and outer forces of evil abound. They strive incessantly to weaken our search for Christian maturity. When others fail, we are not to fret excessively over their misfortune. They have to work out their problems with God, and so do we. All of us are sinners in need of redemption.

God permits this kind of stumbling to exercise and prove us. Demonic seductions and temptations, together with our own obsessions, make us all the more mindful of our need for forgiveness. They prove the error of trying to build a spiritual life on our own merits instead of on the grace of God. As we strive for holy detachment ("denudation") and recollection, we can expect the devil to try to catch us "in one way or another," so that distraction rather than contemplation will rule our inner life.

Forgetful of our need to focus on God (rather than on a particular time or place or person), we will find that our ability to resist the devil's wiles is weakening. Lurking beneath our noblest attempts to mind others' business is the suspicion that if we try hard enough we can reform them to think as we do. Even if we have overcome to a degree our own egocentric willfulness, we may not yet be detached from the collective ego of the community. The naive belief that "we together" can do it entraps us still more securely.

Finally, at the end of these precautions against the world, St. John asks us to consider the words of the Letter of James: "If anyone thinks he is religious and does not bridle tongue, ...his religion is vain" (Jas 1:26).

Expending excessive mental and emotional energy over the affairs of others diminishes our availability to be tranquilly present to God.

It is to this presence that St. John of the Cross wants us to devote ourselves. Every precaution he gives is meant to prepare us for encountering Christ. Whatever the cost, nothing must interfere with this goal. It has to be our first concern. Otherwise our spirituality will be in vain. It will be marked not by peace but by turmoil. We will be at war within ourselves. This inner war of wits and words communicates itself outwardly in agitation, nervousness, unhappiness, and loss of serenity.

Much as we might like to attain inner and outer peace, it seems as if we are always on the way toward it. Still, what counts for us is not success as such but our relaxed intention to try to surrender our heart to Jesus in all things. Then our inner tranquility cannot but show itself outwardly.

> Peace I leave with you; my peace I give to you. Not as the world gives do I give it to you. (Jn 14:27, NAB)

> I give you a new commandment: love one another. As I have loved you, so you also should love one another. This is how all will know that you are my disciples, if you have love for one another. (Jn 13:34-35, NAB)

Our very being will radiate the peace and joy we experience in God's presence. This recollection is what others remember most of all about us. It is a lasting source of faith, hope, and love in community.

The First Precaution Against the Devil

To introduce this precaution and the two that follow from it, St. John notes that among all the wiles the devil uses to mislead people seeking to live the life of the spirit, the devil's favorite and most effective ploy is to deceive people "under the appearance of good rather than of evil."

People who have chosen to live a religious life are hardly likely to commit overtly evil acts. What seduces them and what should arouse their suspicions are things that appear to be good, especially things "not obliged by obedience." When we do the seemingly right thing for the wrong reason, we provide an opening in our character through which the devil can slip. If we do not nip this tendency in the bud by taking the safe path of proper counsel, we may be lost.

Sister Carol Ann is absolutely positive that she is responding to God's call despite questions to the contrary from her religious superiors. After consultation with a "spiritual friend," she feels she has no choice but to leave her community. Paul, a dedicated social worker, swept up in a movement to help the poor, risks his life in the inner city despite the protests of his wife and children. Pastor Michaels, enthralled by the response he receives from his congregation when he preaches, sets himself apart from his peers. He implies to the people that the other pastors do not share his vision, but that God has declared *him* a true prophet.

All of these folks have lofty ideas and ideals. Their original motivations seemed pure, but pride prevented them from questioning the potential evil inherent in even the best of intentions. We must never underestimate the perverting power of the demonic. Any obsession of ours provides an opening to our second enemy. Hence the first precaution:

> 11. Let, then, the first precaution be that, without the command of obedience, you never take upon yourself any work—apart from the obligations of your state—however good and full of charity it may seem, whether for yourself or for anyone else inside or outside the house. By such a practice you will win merit and security, avoid possession, and flee from harm and evils unknown to you, for God will one day demand an account. If you do not observe this precaution in little things as well as big, you will be unable to avoid the devil's deceiving you to a small or great degree, no matter how right you think you are. Even if your negligence amounts to no more than not being governed by obedience in all things, you culpably err, since God wants obedience more than sacrifice [1 Sm 15:22]. The actions of religious are not their own, but belong to obedience, and if you withdraw them from obedience, you will have to count them as lost.

Notice the importance St. John places on obedience. This obligation to listen to legitimate authority keeps self-assurance and self-indulgence in check. Obedience might have saved Sister Carol Ann, Paul, and Pastor Michaels from a great deal of trouble. Anyone who dared to question their good and charitable ways was dubbed automatically wrong. How could the people over them question the work of God they were doing?

By contrast, people who are suspicious of themselves to such a degree that they welcome submission to wise and experienced guides are better able to spot and resist demonic seduction. St. John implies that obedience is like preventative medicine. When we take a hearty dose, it stops a variety of harms unknown to us for which God will one day demand an accounting.

We benefit most from this first precaution against the devil if we observe it in "little things as well as big." The examples already offered involve major life decisions, but what about the times we insist on our own rightness, or copy others' ideas without telling them, or invent so many stories to cover our divisive tracks that we can't recall what is true or false?

These self-deceptions attract the demonic as exposed food attracts flies. If our guard goes down, the devil is as ready to pounce on us as a vulture on weakened prey. The best defense we have is obedience in all things; anything less causes us culpably to err.

We need only to look to Jesus to realize that what God wants most of us is obedience. As far as St. John is concerned, religious who break this vow and become authorities unto themselves might as well be counted as lost. The autarchic nature of pride—which creates a world unto itself—will be almost impossible to resist.

The Second Precaution Against the Devil

If obedience is preventative medicine for the soul aiming to please God, then humility is a sign that we are becoming well. This second precaution sets up as a strong defender against the demonic a good superior—whether a spiritual director, a supervisor on the assembly line, a true friend, a spouse in whom we invest authority over us, or the church itself.

By the sheer fact that we are submissive, we block the relentless tactics of our second enemy, who hates humility in any form. The devil will do anything in his power to steer us wrongly in this regard. One recognizable way the devil uses to erode legitimate authority is to make us question a superior's character, behavior, or ability.

As far as Sister Carol was concerned, her superior was below par intellectually and hopelessly out of touch with the times. Paul could not bear it when his wife, with no background in social work, dared to question his judgment. Pastor Michaels stopped going to ministerial meetings because obviously preachers less skilled than he were jealous of his success.

All three people transferred their allegiance, so to speak, from divinely appointed authority to their own human wisdom. Because they disapproved of the "visible traits" of the people trying to advise them, they lost sight of the "invisible God" whom they thought they were trying to serve. Instead they fell into the devil's trap.

St. John puts the problem succinctly:

> 12. Let the second precaution be that you always look on the superior as though on God, no matter who he happens to be, for he takes God's place. And note that the devil, humility's enemy, is a great and crafty meddler in this area. Much profit and gain come from considering the superior in this light, but serious loss and harm lie in not doing so. Watch, therefore, with singular care that you not dwell on your superior's character, mode of behavior, ability, or any other methods of procedure, for you will so harm yourself as to change your obedience from divine to human, being motivated only by the visible traits of the superior, and not by the invisible God whom you serve through him.
>
> Your obedience is vain and all the more fruitless in the measure that you allow the superior's unpleasant character to annoy you or his good and pleasing manners to make you happy. For I tell you that by inducing religious to consider these modes of conduct, the devil has ruined a vast number of them in their journey toward perfection. Their acts of obedience are worth little in God's sight, since they allow these considerations to interfere with obedience.
>
> If you do not strive, with respect to your personal feelings, to be unconcerned about whether this one or another be superior, you will by no means be a spiritual person, nor will you keep your vows well.

We need not doubt that St. John knew the difference between authoritarian types—boorish, cruel, threatening tyrants—whom he could not abide, and people appointed to the position of superior who were trying to do their best. Not to show them respect is to risk the consequence of demonic divisiveness and the destruction of a community as God's work of art.

Religious houses, to say nothing of family homes or office settings, have crumbled from within because people under a prior, a parent, or a boss never stopped analyzing his or her conduct. Picking apart people in authority, knowing better than they what to do, marks the beginning of the end of many potentially good works.

Our "journey toward perfection" bogs down like boots in fresh tar if we focus more on who says what to us than on maintaining "holy indifference" and going about our work. If there is one barrier the devil cannot penetrate it is that of humble obedience to people invested with proper authority.

The Third Precaution Against the Devil

> 13. The third precaution, directly against the devil, is that you ever seek with all your heart to humble yourself in word and in deed, rejoicing in the good of others as if it were your own, desiring that they be given precedence over you in all things; and this you should do wholeheartedly. You will thereby overcome evil with good [Rom 12:21], banish the devil, and possess a happy heart. Try to practice this more with those who least attract you. Realize that if you do not train yourself in this way, you will not attain real charity or make any progress in it. And ever prefer to be taught by all rather than desire to teach even the least of all.

Having described the ideal climate in which "the devil is prowling...looking for [someone] to devour" (cf. 1 Pt 5:8), St. John of the Cross offers a formula to safeguard ourselves directly from his deceits. I'd like to reformulate his astute advice in a series of imperatives:

> 1. Seek with all your heart to remain humble in word and deed.
> 2. Be large-hearted, capable of offering praise to deserving persons. Don't be envious.

3. Rejoice when something good happens to another person the same as if it were happening to you.

4. Hope that others will be seen as better than you are in all things. Think of yourself as small and inconsequential as compared to them. Don't be jealous.

5. If you do all of the above with genuine good will, you shall overcome evil, banish your second enemy, and be a happy person.

John's point in all of this is to prevent any opening in our character into which the demons of pride, avarice, lust, and envy can slip. Our best defense is to practice these precautions religiously and to direct the same imperatives to people who are the least attractive to us. In this way we can be sure our good will is not whimsical but willing to obey.

The training St. John asks us to undergo is rigorous, because the enemy with whom we must do battle is formidable. In this case, forewarned is forearmed. Unless we learn to appreciate people in authority—even if they are not perfect—we cannot grow in humility, detachment, and fraternal charity. Our progress on the way of perfection, as St. Teresa of Avila would agree, will be minimal to nonexistent. We must be as vigilant and attentive as a strategic planner assessing the battlefield.

At every moment we are in danger of succumbing to the foe. Imagine how confused our enemy will be when we sincerely prefer "to be taught by all rather than desire to teach even the least of all." Such self-effacement is a weapon as powerful as the stone in David's slingshot that downed with one swift blow a giant the size of Goliath (cf.1 Sam 17:1-37).

The First Precaution
Against Oneself and the Shrewdness of Sensuality

Our third enemy is close to home. It is ourself. Its tactic is hard to recognize because nothing is shrewder than selfish sensuality when it comes to displeasing God. How do we deal with this foe?

15. The first precaution is to understand that you have come to the monastery so that all may fashion you and try you. Thus, to free yourself from the imperfections and disturbances that can be engendered by the mannerisms and attitudes of the religious and draw profit from every occurrence, you should think that all in the community are artisans—as indeed they are—present there in order to prove you; that some will fashion you with words, others by deeds, and others with thoughts against you; and that in all this you must be submissive as is the statue to the craftsman who molds it, to the artist who paints it, and to the gilder who embellishes it. If you fail to observe this precaution, you will not know how to overcome your sensuality and feelings, nor will you get along well in the community with the religious or attain holy peace or free yourself from many stumbling blocks and evils.

This first precaution reminds us of the advice St. John offers the community in his *Counsels to a Religious on How to Reach Perfection.* There he will speak of the need for resignation. Here he appeals to the power of formative memory. He asks religious, and, by implication, anyone of us who has made a commitment to our profession, family, church, society, or community, to remember that we have come into this situation not for the sake of self-aggrandizement but to serve God.

To purify our intention, we have to remember that, as the saying goes, God never promised us a rose garden. The people with whom we live and work will try our patience to the nth degree. They will see through our bids for attention. They will take us down from our self-made thrones. They will see to it that we have enough trouble to remain citizens of an imperfect world.

We can be at ease and actually profit from this "formative fashioning" if we remember one thing: God sends these bothersome brothers and sisters into our life as "artisans" to shape us into better persons. An old friend we both love and hate shapes us for the better when he or she uses the sharp tools of words like "Stop feeling so sorry for yourself!"

The co-worker whose desk is nearest to ours does things that annoy us and try our patience, like constantly clearing his throat. The customers whom we serve as a pharmaceutical representative harbor thoughts about us that are not true. They think we are cheating them. They talk behind our back when we have no other recourse—due to a promise of confidentiality—than to remain silent.

In these and myriad other ways of interrelating in community and the marketplace, God is trying to tell us something. When John says that we are to be "submissive," he does not mean that we should ever submit to gross or subtle forms of violence or abuse. Here resistance is the only response.

In this precaution, however, he uses the analogy of artistic endeavor to remind us that new forms and meanings may emerge when we let God do the molding through others' hands. Then the friend who knows us so well is like a craftsman remodeling an old house to release its original beauty. Co-workers become eccentric artists we need in our life to remind us that patience is a hard won virtue. Our customers' suspicions are like rough polishing cloths smoothing the edges of an antique cup. They help us to remain honest in our dealings even when, because of delicate circumstances, we are obliged to withhold some information until full disclosure is possible.

These common examples make clear that if we become too touchy about what other people say or do we will have no peace. Our too-sensitive nature will react rather than respond to changing times and people. It will be impossible for us to flow with the ups and downs of community life. Thus we open ourselves to "many stumbling blocks and evils."

The Second Precaution
Against Oneself and the Shrewdness of Sensuality

If the previous precaution dealt with our feelings this one deals with our doings:

> 16. The second precaution is that you should never give up your works because of a want of satisfaction and delight in them, if they are fitting for the service of God. Neither should you carry out these works merely because of the satisfaction or delight they accord you, but you should do them just as you would the

disagreeable ones. Otherwise it will be impossible for you to gain constancy and conquer your weakness.

The Lord may bless us with the kind of labor we love but, even then, there is no guarantee that what we do will be a sheer delight. There is an element of drudgery in every human endeavor. If our only motivation for delivering the goods is self-gratification, we shall probably not remain a dedicated doer.

To overcome this shrewd trait of sensuality, St. John suggests that we bracket our "want of satisfaction" as a main motive for production. If our labor is intense and sincere, if it is done ultimately to serve God, the fruits will be obvious.

We will not give up a work or carry it out because it pleases our ambition but because it gives glory to God. Then the disagreeable aspects built into any task are not a problem. We take them in stride, remain constant in our commitment, and conquer, with the help of grace, yet another flaw in our character.

The Third Precaution
Against Oneself and the Shrewdness of Sensuality

From feeling and doing, the affective and effective dimensions of our personality, St. John moves to the transcendent level, focusing specifically on the interior life:

> 17. The third precaution is that the interior person should never set eyes on the pleasant feelings found in spiritual exercises, becoming attached to them and carrying out these practices only for the sake of this satisfaction. Nor should such a person run from the bitterness that may be found in them, but rather seek the arduous and distasteful and embrace it. By this practice, sensuality is held in check; without this practice you will never lose self-love or gain the love of God.

In a word, the saint directs us to move beyond the need for consolations in prayer and other spiritual exercises. These pleasant sensations come and go, like good and bad weather. They are not reliable indicators of our progress in the life of the spirit.

To take them as pointers is to make a major mistake. Self-satis-
faction then becomes our gauge for growth, not the mysterious
workings of grace.

Whether God consoles us or withholds any sign of affection
ought not to make a difference. It is better to embrace the bitterness of a desert experience, in which profound inner purification
may be happening, than to run to an oasis of old comforts. By letting God do the leading, we keep in check our sensual desires to run
from the first sign of aridity. This is an essential step on the way to
spiritual maturity.

What St. John offers as the conclusion of this precaution applies to all those we have previously read: "without [these practices]
you will never lose self-love or gain the love of God." Consider this
to be sound advice from an excellent physician of souls. Take to
heart every precaution he recommends. In a short time, you will
notice how much your physical, emotional, mental, and spiritual
well-being improve.

And, as if that were not benefit enough, the beauty of this
health plan is that St. John of the Cross has no intention of sending
you a bill!

The Counsels of St. John of the Cross: Wisdom for Today

St. John's *Counsels to a Religious on How to Reach Perfection* may astound modern ears attuned to pop psychology, radio and television talk shows, self-actualizing life styles, and "new age" spirituality. The advice of some psychologists and sociologists would sound as foreign to St. John's ears as his counsels may sound to ours.

Contemporary spiritual directors may shy away from the task of reinterpreting these texts, but that would be to everyone's loss. The *Counsels* are a valuable resource for persons seeking reliable guidance on the way to God.

In his autobiographical account, *The Sign of Jonas,* Thomas Merton writes:

> I prepared for profession by praying over the *Cautions* and *Counsels* of Saint John of the Cross. For the rest of my religious life I would like, by keeping these *Counsels,* to dispose myself for the work God wants to do in me and to which I am now completely consecrated. They are very simple, the *Cautelas.* It is because they are simple that they are difficult. They do not leave you a chance to compromise. And so it probably takes a lifetime to clear away the obstacles they are designed to remove. Nevertheless they seem to me to be the most detailed and concrete and practical set of rules for arriving at religious perfection that I have ever seen. From a certain point of view they may seem cold and negative. I think, however, that they can be taken as

complementing Saint Benedict's chapter, *De Zelo Bono* [Rule of Saint Benedict, chapter 72, "On the Good Zeal Which Monks Should Have"].[2]

As Merton admits, on first reading the *Counsels* may appear "cold and negative," but let us move beyond this initial, erroneous impression and, as spiritual readers, open ourselves to the deeper wisdom the *Counsels* contain for today.

Reaching Perfection

St. John is under no illusion on this point. Reaching perfection is not a project of self-salvation but a work of grace. We are to stand before God as we are, with our faults and failings, our sins and imperfections. The *Counsels* presuppose that one has undergone a deep conversion experience, a real *metanoia,* a turning of our lives over to God.

Speaking as a wise, learned, and experienced director of souls, with the right balance of gentleness and firmness, the saint addresses contemplative religious living in community. Specifically he wants to guide a friar (whom he calls "Your Charity"[3]) to new heights of conformity to Christ. His words are applicable to anyone who desires to be united with the Beloved. Their relevance extends far beyond the walls of a monastery or convent. The wisdom of the *Counsels* is of perennial value to laity as well as religious.

St. John wrote this minor work sometime between 1585 and 1587. He composed the *Counsels* in short order, probably under pressure, because he was occupied with business and travel as Vicar Provincial. His intention was to give the friar a short formula for abiding always in God's presence, whatever external circumstances might prevail. A formative reading of these directives reveals, by implication, that they have something to say to all Christians. A condition for heeding his advice is peaceful receptivity; the result is a being led inevitably to the passion. St. John had no illusions about this point. To accept Christ as the center of our lives is to shoulder our cross.

Merton journals about the same theme in *The Sign of Jonas:*

October 7 [1949]

Spiritual joy depends on the cross. Unless we deny ourselves, we will find ourselves in everything and that is misery. As soon as we begin to deny ourselves, out of love for God, we begin to find God, at least obscurely. Since God is our joy, our joy is proportioned to our self-denial, for the love of God. I say: our self-denial for the love of God, because there are people who deny themselves for love of themselves.

It is not complicated, to lead the spiritual life. But it is difficult. We are blind, and subject to a thousand illusions. We must expect to be making mistakes almost all the time. We must be content to fall repeatedly and to begin again to try to deny ourselves, for the love of God.

It is when we are angry at our own mistakes that we tend most of all to deny ourselves for love of ourselves. We want to shake off the hateful thing that has humbled us. In our rush to escape the humiliation of our own mistakes, we run head first into the opposite error, seeking comfort and compensation. And so we spend our lives running back and forth from one attachment to another.

If that is all our self-denial amounts to, our mistakes will never help us.

The thing to do when you have made a mistake is not to give up doing what you were doing and start something altogether new, but to start over again with the thing you began badly and try, for the love of God, to do it well.[4]

To spend time trying to justify our failures is futile. What counts is not the success we enjoy but the fact that we keep on trying to do good, no matter how often we fail. To live these counsels in inner peace is to accept that we are going to make mistakes. We may betray our best intentions, but words like these call us back to the joy of self-denial long after selfish gains have led to disappointment.

The *Counsels* do not offer us goals we can expect to reach overnight. They present us with ongoing tasks and challenges. The aim of the *Counsels* is not to develop a self-sufficient personality but to live in harmony with the will of God. On this earth we will never arrive at the fullness of divine intimacy; we will always be on the way.

The perfection for which we strive here can at most only approximate the glory to come; it cannot contain the fullness of our heart's fondest longing for union with God.

Four Words of Truth

"Your holy Charity" has asked St. John to put a vast amount of teaching into a few words, and so he replies:

> 1. Your holy Charity with few words asked me for a great deal. An answer would require much time and paper. Seeing, then, that I lack both of these, I will try to be concise and jot down only certain points and counsels which in sum will contain much, so that whoever observes them perfectly will attain a high degree of perfection.
>
> The one who wishes to be a true religious and fulfill the promises of the profession that was made to God, advance in virtue, and enjoy the consolations and the delight of the Holy Spirit, will be unable to do so without trying to practice with the greatest diligence the four following counsels, concerning resignation, mortification, the practice of virtue, and bodily and spiritual solitude.

These four words—*resignation, mortification, virtue,* and *solitude*—reflect fundamental spiritual truths that must be put into practice by committed Christians.

The *Counsels* aim to help religious fulfill the promises of their state of life. They are specifications in some sense of the threefold path of obedience, chaste love, and poverty of spirit that constitute the vowed life.[5] Applied to the faithful, obedience means to listen (*ob-audire*) with the inner ear of the heart to God's voice in the here and now circumstances of life. Chaste love suggests manifesting gentle, compassionate concern for all those entrusted to our care. Poverty of spirit invites us to empty ourselves of egocentric desires so that we may seek God as the sole satisfaction of our heart's longing.

The *Counsels* aim to help believers advance in virtue by fulfilling the Father's will as Jesus did. Practicing these four foundations of the faith enables us to enjoy already on earth the consolation and delight of the Holy Spirit, the peace of heart only oneness with God can bring. Though the *Counsels* are directed to contemplative religious, they are timeless in their validity. They are an invaluable resource for fostering Christian character and personality formation. They bring wisdom and balance to community living.

Resignation

> 2. In order to practice the first counsel, concerning resignation, you should live in the monastery as though no one else were in it. And thus you should never, by word or by thought, meddle in things that happen in the community, nor with individuals in it, desiring not to notice their good or bad qualities or their conduct. And in order to preserve your tranquillity of soul, even if the whole world crumbles, you should not desire to advert to this or interfere, remembering Lot's wife who was changed into hard stone because she turned her head to look at those who in the midst of much clamor and noise were perishing [Gn 19:26].
>
> You should practice this with great fortitude, for you will thereby free yourself from many sins and imperfections and guard the tranquility and quietude of your soul with much profit before God and others.
>
> Ponder this often, because it is so important that, for not observing it, many religious not only failed to improve their other works of virtue and religious observance, but ever slipped back from bad to worse.

All of us have an urge to know what is happening around us. We are curious. What others are doing and saying is of interest to us. We want information: Where are they going? With whom? Why? When? Our aim, at least overtly, is not to meddle in their lives but merely to know the latest information.

Such speculation poses a problem for St. John. It takes seekers out of themselves; it breaks their concentrated attention to God. Once idle curiosity takes precedence over prayer, it can give rise to petty envy and jealousy, especially in the close confines of a community.

In the secluded atmosphere of a contemplative monastery, religious can begin to focus more on their mutual attractions and aversions than on Christ. Gossip can buzz around like flies in an open-air restaurant. In this situation, priests, brothers, or sisters can get emotionally involved in one another's business, meddling all the time.

For this reason, St. John cautions us to stay aloof from gossip, to remain composed, even if the whole world were to crumble. This is what he means by the word *resignation*. We are dying to know what is going on, we are consumed with curiosity, yet we resign ourselves to not knowing. Our feverish imagination proposes a thousand reasons why we should know, but against this onslaught, we resign ourselves to the wisdom of our original call to love and serve God with our whole heart, mind, and will. As long as we do not tackle the deeply rooted fault of consuming curiosity, other obstacles related to it will rise whenever we live in proximity to one another.

In family, dormitory, office, or community, problems related to meddling may abound. All of us are tempted to poke into the privacy of other people's business. We are prone to form power groups and gossipy cliques, often for the ostensible good of another person, but the results can be disastrous. We can destroy a person's reputation by subtle innuendo. We steal the other's right to live in community in peace. Worse than this, we mask violence as love. Our aim is not concern but control of a family, school, organization, or community.

These are only a few of the problems that can arise if we do not overcome the deformative "sins and imperfections" associated with the loss of tranquility. The practice of resignation is to be modulated in accordance with each person's situation. In some situations (as, for example, in positions of authority), a person needs to know, not to satisfy his or her curiosity but because of the leadership role one plays.

Nevertheless, St. John is aware of the loss of quietude that can happen in a community if members do not temper unwarranted curiosity by spiritual resignation. They may be besieged by manipulative or seductive relationships, distracted by a sickly "peeping Tom" mentality, and overcome by inner clamor.

The spiritual resignation of not knowing does not mean a forced retreat from facts. What it entails is more a gentle catching of ourselves interiorly when we begin to feel caught in a net of unnecessary worry, destructive gossip, and undue meddling; when we become so preoccupied with this or that plan or project that we forget the primacy of the love relationship that ought to exist between us and God.

The busier we are about the business of others—seeing the sliver in their eyes and missing the plank in our own (cf. Mt 7:3)—the more likely we are to backslide from bad to worse. We are not at peace with ourselves, others, or God. If we do not modify the habit of idle curiosity, it will harm our decisions and actions. Peace departs from us faster than water flowing over a dam if we live in inner tension, agitation, turmoil, and nervousness. We cannot possibly be as efficient in our task or as responsive to the needs of others as we should be.

We must, with God's grace, strive to find resignation of soul out of which we can radiate the joy, gentleness, patience, and kindness that are the fruits of Christian living. If we are able, through grace and our own efforts, to find that inner core of peace, then life goes on in a more gracious manner. The same duties are done. The same effective work is accomplished, but the atmosphere around us remains courteous, not curious. Persons practice charity and compassion toward one another rather than contempt and competition.

Curiosity disrupts resignation. It creates an untranquil atmosphere of in-groups versus out-groups. Invasion of privacy, meddling, envious comparison, backbiting, and other signs of communal turmoil spoil family, professional, and religious life. Everyone loses. No one profits when pettiness replaces prayerfulness.

If we practice the spiritual discipline of stopping the train of curiosity before it starts, especially during trying circumstances, we will free ourselves from many impediments to grace and guard the quietude of soul St. John of the Cross values so highly.

If we can grow gradually in the attitude of returning to God in peaceful resignation when turmoil abounds, we shall soon reestablish inner tranquillity. Out of this quiet center there flows our doing of daily tasks. No time is wasted on consuming curiosity.

This balance of inner quietude and outer efficiency is the formula for gracious living wherever we find ourselves. Everyone feels happier in such a resigned and respecting atmosphere. We literally reassign to our lives the religious meaning that attracted us to God in the first place.

Mortification

> 3. To practice the second counsel, which concerns mortification, and profit by it, you should engrave this truth on your heart. And it is that you have not come to the monastery for any other reason than to be worked and tried in virtue; you are like the stone that must be chiseled and fashioned before being set in the building.
>
> Thus you should understand that those who are in the monastery are craftsmen placed there by God to mortify you by working and chiseling at you. Some will chisel with words, telling you what you would rather not hear; others by deed, doing against you what you would rather not endure; others by their temperament, being in their person and in their actions a bother and annoyance to you; and others by their thoughts, neither esteeming nor feeling love for you.
>
> You ought to suffer these mortifications and annoyances with inner patience, being silent for love of God and understanding that you did not enter the religious life for any other reason than for others to work you in this way, and so that you become worthy of heaven. If this was not your reason for entering the religious state, you should not have done so, but should have remained in the world to seek your comfort, honor, reputation, and ease.

Consider the call of a Thomas Merton. If he weren't motivated to give himself to God in total fidelity, why would he have entered a monastic community in the first place? If he became a Trappist for any other reason, for instance, to be praised or to seek special status, it would have been better for him to stay in the world. Those who people the monastery with him are part of God's plan for his life. Some of them will, to be sure, inspire him to be a good monk, but others will mold and fashion him in ways that may hurt before they help. His task throughout the lifelong process of always ongoing formation is to live first and foremost for God and in the sight of God.

It is easy to apply this counsel to contemplatives, but does it speak to people in the world? We know from experience that human relations are not easy. Nothing chisels and fashions us quite as much as close contact with other people, who seem to specialize in grinding away at our grandiosity.

We have no choice about our place of birth or our parents. We find ourselves surrounded by teachers, friends, peers, and rivals who chip away at us like sculptors on marble. Guardians and persons in authority mold us from youth to old age. So do casual acquaintances and even perfect strangers. Mean or cutting remarks crack our composure. We long for kindness but we are often met by a grumpy morning face. We seek confirmation and receive instead a snide remark others do not realize we have overheard. A promise unkept can ruin our day, a betrayal of fidelity our entire life.

Each failure in human relationships reminds us anew of our dependence on God. Others' words tell us what we hate to hear. Their deeds try our patience. Their temperaments test our endurance. The admonition of friends humbles our arrogance. Their pointed criticism reminds us that we are far away from the relaxed give-and-take we seek. Through these chiseling interactions, we grow in the awareness that perfect friendship and trust may only be possible with God.

By means of such annoyances, we die daily to self-centeredness. This is the meaning of spiritual mortification. Through the fashioning, molding, chiseling, and grinding powers of others whom God lets us encounter for his purposes, we become more the self he wants us to be. A necessary part of spiritual growth is to be refined in fire. Only then can grace release, as does a skilled wood carver, the unique "life forms" we have been called to be from the beginning.

Daily dying to egocentric desires diminishes unrealistic expectations of what family or community should be or do for us. No human group in and of itself can fulfill us. No matter what we do to build or create community, it can never fully meet our expectations.

Human beings in their unpredictability will always be there to chisel us with bad tempers, unexpected conflicts, petty tensions.

The community St. John of the Cross addresses is not a community of saints but of sinners. Our only salvation is to center our attention on God, not on others. Loving the Lord above all else allows us to relativize good and bad community relations. We keep our sense of humor and live in humility. Such realism tempers any utopian ideal that we can find a perfect community or that we can build or create one.

Growth in inner patience is the fruit of such mortification. We die daily to false expectations. We accept the "craftsmen" God sends into our lives. When their chiseling with words, deeds, temperamental differences, or pejorative thoughts annoys us, we turn to the Holy Spirit instead of flying off the handle. Rather than seeking to defend ourselves, we are silent for the love of God. We used to push to get our point across; now we pray for the grace of patience that we may be worthy of heaven.

We welcome the mortification that helps us to remember that God has placed us in this situation not to give us worldly "comfort, honor, reputation, and ease" but to enable our spiritual growth. If we are patient and trust God to take care of things, the fruit of this dying process will be new life in the Lord.

> 4. The second counsel is wholly necessary for religious so they may fulfill the obligations of their state and find genuine humility, inward quietude, and joy in the Holy Spirit. If you do not practice this, you will know neither how to be a religious nor even why you came to the religious life. Neither will you know how to seek Christ (but only yourself), or find peace of soul, or avoid sinning and often feeling troubled.
>
> Trials will never be lacking in religious life, nor does God want them to be. Since he brings souls there to be proved and purified, like gold, with hammer and the fire [Sir 2:5], it is fitting that they encounter trials and temptations from human beings and from devils, and the fire of anguish and affliction.
>
> The religious must undergo these trials, and should endeavor to bear them patiently and in conformity to God's will, and not so sustain them that instead of being approved by God

in this affliction he be reproved for not having wanted to carry the cross of Christ in patience.

Since many religious do not understand that they have entered religious life to carry Christ's cross, they do not get along well with others. At the time of reckoning they will find themselves greatly confused and frustrated.

"Humility, inward quietude, and joy in the Holy Spirit" are the first fruits of a God-guided life. We need to grow in the conviction that trials, anguish, affliction, and suffering are not deliberately mean or arbitrary tests God sends but aids to the inner purification of the will that all true lovers of the Lord must undergo. Carrying our cross can take many forms. For some people the cross may involve physical pain (the purification of passive, patient endurance); for others it may mean practicing charity in community in generous acts of service (the purification of active, intentional effectiveness). In either case, the glory belongs to God.

Our goal is to seek Christ, not self-gratification, to find peace, not its pretense in a false sense of security. Sin is impossible to avoid unless we focus on our crucified, risen Lord and use every occasion of suffering Providence allows to work out our salvation. The goal of purification is not to make us feel troubled but together, not disjointed but united with Christ. Those who make a serious commitment to follow him ought to expect trials. As St. John says, "[they] will never be lacking" in any walk of life. Only if our faith is strong will we be able to inspire others. To carry our cross in patience amidst these trials and temptations strengthens conformity to Christ.

When the pharisees tried to trick Jesus, he stood his ground and preached the truth. He remained as humble and obedient to the Father's will as a lamb brought to slaughter, but he was wise enough to resist every tactic the devil used to dissuade him from his call. Christ endured anguish and affliction to stay faithful, and so must we. As he shows us, the path to peace is paved with stones of purgation.

Daily life brings trials enough, according to our state of life. We do not have to seek them. A time of reckoning will come. How shall we respond? John contends that we will be held accountable for our deeds. God is not an unmerciful judge, but a loving father who wants us to grow strong in the faith by accepting the demands it places on us.

If our goal in life is getting along with others by following the pressures of the crowd, we will never conform to Christ. When the time comes to answer to him for our choices, what will we say? When the day of reckoning is upon us, how will we respond?

This counsel alerts us to what ultimately counts. It teaches us how to avoid confusion. It shows us how to diminish frustration and advance in faith.

Practice of Virtue

5. To practice the third counsel, which concerns the practice of virtue, you should be constant in your religious observance and in obedience without any concern for the world, but only for God. In order to achieve this and avoid being deceived, you should never set your eyes on the satisfaction or dissatisfaction of the work at hand as a motive for doing it or failing to do it, but on doing it for God. Thus you must undertake all things, agreeable or disagreeable, for the sole purpose of pleasing God through them.

6. To do this with fortitude and constancy and acquire the virtues quickly, you should take care always to be inclined to the difficult more than to the easy, to the rugged more than to the soft, to the hard and distasteful in a work more rather than to its delightful and pleasant aspects; and do not go about choosing what is less a cross, for the cross is a light burden [Mt 11:30]. The heavier a burden is, the lighter it becomes when borne for Christ.

You should try, too, by taking the lowest place always, that in things bringing comfort to your brothers in religion they be preferred to you. This you should do wholeheartedly, for it is the way to becoming greater in spiritual things, as God tells us in his Gospel: *Qui se humiliaverit exaltabitur* [Mt. 23:12].

Upon entering the Trappists, Thomas Merton expected to forsake the concerns of ordinary life in the world and to take up a new way of being inside the monastery. His life would be oriented solely around pleasing God through prayer and labor. He learned that a monk can scrub a floor, answer the door, milk a cow, or make jelly for the love of God, whether this task satisfies him personally or not.

Again this counsel applies not only to contemplatives but to every Christian. The practice of virtue builds character. We are constant, not fickle, ready for Christ's sake to perform good deeds with ease, to be consistent in our religious observances, to be obedient to God's will in each situation. The satisfaction or dissatisfaction we receive from doing a work is not the reason we do it. Our motivation is freer than that. Agreeable or not, we do what we must for the sole motive of pleasing God. This was the secret of the "little way of spiritual childhood" practiced so faithfully by saints like Brother Lawrence of the Resurrection and Thérèse of Lisieux.

One way to practice virtue with "fortitude and constancy"—the way Christ taught by word and deed—is to do what is contrary to the world's expectations: not the easy way out but the difficult pursuit of excellence; not the "soft sell" but the rugged way of long hours and strict dedication; not a penchant for the pleasant or for what pays more, but a willingness to work hard to make something right, even if the labor demanded is distasteful.

If all we seek are delightful side benefits, we will never understand how ultimately light the cross is when we bear it for the Lord's sake. When was the last time we took the lowest place? How often instead do we prefer things that bring us comfort, honor, and ease?

We facilitate the practice of this third counsel when we do what we do for God, and not for the reward we may or may not receive. After a while, we may even be "inclined" to choose the difficult, the rugged, the distasteful, not as an exercise in masochism or self-mastery but as the way to form our character in imitation of Christ.

This counsel directs us away from mere vital pleasures or personal gains toward the goal of pleasing God and bearing joyfully for his sake whatever crosses we have to carry. Growth in fortitude and constancy implies becoming detached interiorly from satisfaction or dissatisfaction as our main aim. If these pleasant or unpleasant experiences occur, we take them in stride, but we do not make them the main motive for what we do or do not decide. Rather we set our eyes on Christ. His way has to be our own.

As we grow in the art and discipline of detaching ourselves from feelings of loss or gain, we begin to attach ourselves to the attitude of doing what we do, pleasant or unpleasant, delightful or distasteful, solely for the love of God.

A key question remains to be asked: How do we reconcile this counsel with the legitimate striving of persons in the world for promotion, for deserved salary increments, for a better place to live?

The Christian spiritual life, with its emphasis on incarnational spirituality, does not exclude the possibility that what we do will, in fact, give us pleasure, just remuneration, and satisfaction; it only excludes making such motives ultimate. Otherwise persons might choose to care only for those rich in material goods and neglect those who are poor. Christian care extends to both classes.

Once our motivation is rooted in the love of God, we are liberated interiorly to do whatever is asked of us without the provision of having always to be praised for it or having always to derive personal pleasure from it. If such praise and pleasure come, we thank God for these gifts, but we do not make the rewards promised to us conditions for doing or not doing what is necessary.

When St. John of the Cross writes that we are to follow the difficult rather than the easy road, he is addressing those who have chosen to imitate Christ whatever their state of life. Jesus took the rugged path because it led to our redemption. However heavy the cross Christ asks us to carry, it becomes light when we lift it with and for him. By taking up our daily crosses joyfully, by doing our duty wholeheartedly, without concentrating on personal gain, we grow in the virtues and dispositions that ought to characterize strong Christians. We become humble servants, worthy of being exalted by God.

Solitude

7. To practice the fourth counsel, which concerns solitude, you should deem everything in the world as finished. Thus, when (for not being able to avoid it) you have to deal with some matter, do so in as detached a way as you would if it did not exist.

8. Pay no heed to the things out in the world, for God has already withdrawn and released you from them. Do not handle any business yourself that you can do through a third person. It is very fitting for you to desire to see no one and that no one see you.

And note carefully that if God will ask a strict account from all the faithful of every idle word, how much more will he ask it of religious who have consecrated all their life and works to him. And God will demand all of this on the day of reckoning.

This fourth counsel is a further specification of the first one on resignation. There we were told not to be curious, not to get involved in what does not pertain to us. No matter how secluded our lives are, there arise matters of business to which we must attend. The question is, can we do so in a way that helps rather than hinders spiritual living?

The key phrase here seems to be "do so in as detached a way as you would if [the world] did not exist." This phrase seems to be a warning, valid for all, against getting absorbed in our work to the exclusion of God. We must guard against allowing worldly cares to penetrate into the center of our heart where God alone should reign.

To live and work in the world as if it did not exist does not mean ceasing to act; it means steering clear of the grip of over-involvement. In the world, we cannot avoid seeing people, but is it possible that we overdo our social involvements to the detriment of our spiritual life? Do we not use idle, damaging, uncharitable words so much that our tongue is like the small flame that sets fire to a huge forest (cf. Jas 3:5)?

We must not conclude from this call to solitude that we can get away with doing a careless job. St. John of the Cross warns against this false assumption. The secret is to do as well as possible what we have to do but, when it is finished, to treat our accomplishment as if it were unimportant. How do we attain such detachment without falling into excessive denial of the world? The answer, in a word, is "solitude."

Solitude is an essential condition for any spiritual deepening whatsoever, whether we live in the world or a monastery. The more incarnational we are, the more we will realize that God is appealing to us in persons, events, and things in our workaday world.

Solitude enables us to see their epiphanic meaning from the perspective of our time alone with God. We must try, wherever we are—whether in a busy bus depot or on the beach—to quiet ourselves inwardly, to put worldly cares aside momentarily and to pay attention solely to our loving Lord.

This attitude of inner quieting affects our dealings in the business world. In solitude, we can begin to appreciate this world and the goodness of its creation. At the same time, we acknowledge peacefully that all is passing.

By releasing our frantic grasp on the world's goods, we learn to use them wisely. If we see the temporal as a manifestation of the eternal, we are less likely to base our dealings on self-gain. If we avoid the snares of emotional intrigue and useless chatter that signify a loss of solitude, we are able to conduct our business more objectively.

Creating inner space also produces the side benefit of preventing impulsive or unwise decisions. If we can act in our affairs in a way that tempers grasping, aggressive attitudes, we are better able to discover the best course of action. We will as a rule take into account what Christ would say or do.

The condition that most facilitates such freeing solitude and provides many of the benefits described in the fourth counsel is prayer. Authentic prayer never leads to the neglect of participation. Like leisure, it enhances labor. Contemplation is the soil out of which sound action emerges.

> 9. I do not mean here that you fail to fulfill the duties of your state with all necessary and possible care, and any others that obedience commands, but that you execute your tasks in such a way that no fault is committed, for neither God nor obedience wants you to commit a fault.
>
> You should consequently strive to be incessant in prayer, and in the midst of your corporal practices do not abandon it. Whether you eat, or drink, or speak, or converse with lay people, or do anything else, you should always do so with the desire for God and with your heart fixed on him. This is very

necessary for inner solitude, which demands that the soul dismiss any thought that is not directed to God. And in forgetfulness of all things that are and happen in this short and miserable life, do not desire to know anything in any way except how better to serve God and keep the observance of your institute.

Unceasing prayer of this sort does not mean mumbling pious sayings from dawn to dusk. Prayer deepens our desire for God. We fix our thoughts and feelings on him so that we do not become fixated on the things of this world as ends in themselves. In this sense, prayer is as necessary to the spirit as breathing is to the body; it is the unbroken (spoken or unspoken) lifting of our hearts and minds to God as he gloriously manifests himself in all of creation.

As a true contemplative, John of the Cross loved the beauty, goodness, and truth he beheld in God's splendid gifts of nature and culture. He never shirked the demands obedience placed upon him—to follow the rough road of the Teresian reform, to accept graciously the blessing and burden of spiritual direction, to write poems and prose works under the most trying circumstances. By the same token, he never neglected prayer. It was as integrated into his religious life as was the water into the wine with which he celebrated the Eucharist.

St. John is not only recommending that we live a life of prayer; he also seems to be saying something bolder, namely, that we are to become living prayer. Eating, drinking, speaking or listening, resting or executing a task, we can pray provided we "do so with desire for God and with [our] heart fixed on him." Thus do we loosen our fearful grasp on this short and passing life and come to enjoy true liberation. For us there is then no break between contemplation and action; one flows from and into the other.

Conclusion

St. John of the Cross concludes the *Counsels* with this short sentence:

10. If your Charity observes these four counsels with care, you will reach perfection in a very short time. These counsels are so

interdependent that if you are lacking in one of them, you will begin to lose the profit and gain you have from practicing the others.

These four directives form a square. If one side is missing, the shape is destroyed. If all are intact, the contours remain visible. If we overcome sickly curiosity by resigning ourselves to the task at hand, we can be more objective in our dealings with others. We will be less prone to follow the swiftly changing likes and dislikes of unreliable gossips. Learning to die daily to self-centeredness enables us to develop good habits of Christian living, like taking the lowest place, being patient, and allowing God, not desires for gain, to determine our degree of commitment. Living in inner solitude fosters prayer, and prayer helps us to forget ourselves. In short, losing one side of the square, we lose them all; gaining one, we gain them all.

On our own we would not be able to follow this rigorous way of perfection. What motivates and guides us is the love of God and the longing of our soul for transforming union. God gives us the grace we need to go the distance. Despite the times we are bombarded by the noise of the world, we find the strength to walk the way of the cross.

Love motivates us over a lifetime of trying to unblock the obstacles that stand in the way of entering wholly into the presence of God. The dispositions of resignation, mortification, practice of virtue, and bodily and spiritual solitude offer us a sound plan for spiritual living. They enable us to grow daily in humility, inner stillness, and joy in the Spirit. These precious gifts may then radiate through us to the people God entrusts to our care. Our lives will become like clear glass through which others can catch a glimpse of the Lord we love.

Notes

1. *Ascent of Mount Carmel,* bk. 1, chap. 13, sec. 11, from *The Collected Works of St. John of the Cross,* trans. Kieran Kavanaugh and Otilio Rodriguez, rev. ed. (Washington, DC: ICS Publications, 1991).

2. Entry for March 20, 1947, from Thomas Merton, *The Sign of Jonas* (Garden City, NY: Doubleday & Co., Image Books, 1956), p. 40.

3. "Your Charity" or "Your holy Charity" were the forms used at the time for addressing friars who were not priests; "your Reverence" was used for priests.

4. Merton, *Sign of Jonas,* p. 236.

5. See Susan Muto and Adrian van Kaam, *Commitment: Key to Christian Maturity* (New York: Paulist Press, 1991).

The Institute of Carmelite Studies promotes research and publication in the field of Carmelite spirituality. Its members are Discalced Carmelites, part of a Roman Catholic community—friars, nuns, and laity—who are heirs to the teaching and way of life of Teresa of Jesus and John of the Cross, men and women dedicated to contemplation and to ministry in the church and the world. Information concerning their way of life is available through local diocesan Vocation Offices, or from the Vocation Director's Office, 1525 Carmel Road, Hubertus, WI, 53033.